A DICTIONARY

OF

SCRIPTURE PROPER NAMES,

WITH

Their Pronunciations and Explanations.

FAIRBANKS & CO.,
54 & 56, MADISON STREET,
CHICAGO, ILLS.

DICTIONARY OF SCRIPTURE PROPER NAMES

WITH THEIR PRONUNCIATION AND MEANINGS.

[NOTE.—*The accent* (') *shows where the stress of the voice should fall.* (?) *denotes meanings which are doubtful.* (q. v.)—"*which see*"—*refer to the word indicated. The diphthong* (ai) *is to be pronounced as in the English word* "*aisle.*"]

AAR

AARON, a'-ron, lofty, mountainous.

ABADDON, a-bad'-don, the destroyer.

ABAGTHA, a-bag'-thah, given by fortune.

ABANA, ab'-a-nah.

ABARIM, ab-a'-rim, regions beyond.

ABBA, ab'-bah, father.

ABDA, ab'-dah, servant.

ABDI, ab'-dy, s. of Jehovah.

ABDIEL, ab'-di-el, s. of God.

ABDON, ab'-don, servile.

ABEDNEGO, a-bed'-ne-go, servant or worshipper of Nego (Mercury ?).

ABEL, a'-bel, vanity, vapour. (2) A meadow.

ABEL-BETH-MAACHAH, a'-bel-beth-ma'-a-kah, meadow of the house of Maachah.

ABEL-MAIM, a'-bel-may'-im, m. of the waters.

ABEL-MEHOLAH, a'-bel-me-ho'-lah, m. of dancing.

ABEL-MIZRAIM, a'-bel-miz'-ray-im, mourning of the Egyptians.

ABEL-SHITTIM, a'-bel-shit'-tim, meadow of acacias.

ABEZ, a'-bez, whiteness.

ABI, ab'-i, } whose father is
ABIAH, ab-i'-ah, } Jehovah.

ABI-ALBON, ab-by-al'-bon, f. of strength.

ABIASAPH, ab-i'-a-saf, f. of gathering.

ABIATHAR, ab-i'-a-thar, f. of plenty.

ABIB, a'-bib, an ear of corn, or green ear.

ABIDAH, ab-i'-dah, father of knowledge.

ABN

ABIDAN, ab'-i-dan, f. of a judge.

ABIEL, ab'-i-el, f. of strength.

ABI-EZER, ab-i-e'-zer, f. of help.

ABIGAIL, ab'-i-gal, whose f. is exultation.

ABIHAIL, ab-i-ha'-il, f. of strength.

ABIHU, a-bi'-hu, He (i. e., God) is my f.

ABIHUD, ab-i'-hud, whose f. is Judah.

ABIJAH, ab-i'-jah, whose f. is Jehovah.

ABIJAM, ab-i'-jam, whose f. is Jehovah.

ABILENE, ab-bi-le'-ne, a grassy place (?).

ABIMAEL, ab-bim'-ma-el, father of might.

ABIMELECH, ab-bim'-me-lek, f. king, or f. of the king.

ABINIDAB, ab-in'-a-dab, noble f., or f. of nobility.

ABINOAM, ab-in'-o-am, f. of pleasantness.

ABIRAM, ab-i'-ram, f. of loftiness.

ABISHAG, ab'-i-shag, whose f. is error (?).

ABISHAI, ab-ish-ai, f. of gift.

ABISHALOM, ab-ish'-a-lom, f. of peace.

ABISHUA, ab-ish'-u-ah, f. of welfare.

ABISHUR, ab'-i-shur, f. of the wall.

ABITAL, ab'-i-tal, whose f. is the dew.

ABITUB, ab'-i-tub, f. of goodness.

ABIUD, ab-i'-hud, f. of praise.

ABNER, ab'-ner, f. of light.

ABRAM, ab'-ram, a high *f.*

ABRAHAM, ab'-ra-ham, *f.* of a great multitude.

ABSALOM, ab'-sa-lom, *f.* of peace.

ACCAD, ak'-kad, fortress.

ACCHO, ak'-ko, sand-heated (by the sun).

ACELDAMA, a-kel'-da-ma, field of blood.

ACHAIA, ak-a'-yah

ACHAICUS, ak-a'-i-kus, belonging to Achaia.

ACHAN, or ACHAR, a'-kan, a'-kar, troubling, or troubled.

ACHAZ, a'-kaz (same as AHAZ, q. v.).

ACHBOR, ak'-bor, a mouse.

ACHIM, a'-kim (perhaps the same as JACHIN, q. v.).

ACHISH, a'-kish, angry (?).

ACHMETHA, ak'-me-thah, fortress (?).

ACHOR, A'-kor, trouble, causing sorrow.

ACHSAH, ak'-sah, anklet.

ACH-SHAPH, ak'-shaf, enchantment.

ACHZIB, ak'-zib, deceit.

ADA, ADAH, a'-dah, ornament, beauty

ADADAH (probably should be Ararah, the same as ARARR, q. v.).

ADAIAH, ad-ai'-yah, whom Jehovah adorns.

ADALIA, ad-al'-i-ah, upright (?).

ADAM, ad'-am,
ADAMA,
ADAMAH, } ad'-a-mah, red, red earth.

ADAMI, ad'-a-my, human.

ADAR, a'-dar, greatness, splendour.

ADBEEL, ad'-be-el, miracle of God.

ADDAN, ad'-dan, humble (?).

ADDAR, ad'-dar, greatness (?).

ADDI, ad'-dy, ornament.

ADDON, ad'-don, humble (?).

ADER, a'-der, flock.

ADIEL, ad'-i-el, ornament of God.

ADIN, a'-din,
ADINA, ad'-i-na, } slender, pliant, delicate.

ADITHAIM, ad-i-thay'-im, twofold ornament, or prey.

ADLAI, ad'-lai, justice of God.

ADMAH, ad'-mah (same as ADAMAH, q. v.).

ADMATHA, ad'-ma-thah, earthy (?).

ADNA,
ADNAH, } ad'-nah, pleasure.

ADONIBEZEK, a-do'-ni-be'-zek, lord of Bezek.

ADONIJAH, ad-o-ni'-jah, Jehovah is my Lord.

ADONIKAM, ad-o-ni'-kam, lord of enemies.

ADONIRAM, ad-o-ni'-ram, *l.* of height.

ADONIZEDEC, a-don'-i-ze'-dek, *l.* of justice.

ADORAIM, ad-o-ray'-im, two heaps of mounds.

ADORAM, a-do'-ram (contracted from ADONIRAM, q. v.).

ADRAMMELECH, ad - ram' - me - lek, magnificence of the king, king of fire.

ADRAMYTTIUM, ad-ra-mit'-ti-um.

ADRIA, a'-dri-ah.

ADRIEL, ad'-ri-el, flock of God.

ADULLAM, ad-ul'-lam, justice of the people.

ADUMMIM, ad-um'-mim, the red (men ?).

ÆNEAS, ee-nee'-as, praised.

ÆNON, ee'-non, springs.

AGABUS, ag'-a-bus, a locust, father's feast.

AGAG, a'-gag, flaming.

AGAR, a'-gar (see HAGAR).

AGEE, ag'-gee, fugitive.

AGRIPPA, a-grip'-pah, one who at his birth causes pain.

AGUR, a'-gur, an assembler, one of the assembly.

AHAB, a'-hab, father's brother.

AHARAH, ah'-a-rah, after the brother.

AHARHEL, a-har'-hel, behind the wall, or breastwork.

AHASAI, a-haz'-ai (probably a contraction of AHAZIAH, q. v.).

AHASBAI, a-haz'-bai, I flee to Jehovah.

AHASUERUS, ahas-u-e'-rus, lion-king, probably the same as XERXES.

AHAVA, a-ha'-vah, water.

AHAZ, a'-haz, possessor.

AHAZIAH, a-ha-zi'-ah, whom Jehovah upholds.

AHBAN, ah'-ban, brother of the wise.

AHER, a'-her, following.

AHI, a'-hi,
AHIAH, ahi'-ah, } brother of Jehovah.

AHIAM, ahi'-am, *b.* of the people.

AHIAN, ahi'-an, brotherly.

AHIEZER, a-hi-e'-zer, brother of help.

AHIHUD, ahi'-hud, *b.* (*i. e.,* friend) of the Jews (or of praise).

AHIJAH, ahi'-jah (same as AHIAH, q. v.).

AHIKAM, ahi'-kam, *b.* of the enemy.

AHILUD, ahi'-lud, *b.* of one born.

AHIMAAZ, ahim'-a-az, *b.* of anger.

AHIMAN, ahi'-man, brother of a gift.

AHIMELECH, ahim'-me-lek, b. of the king.
AHIMOTH, ahi'-moth, b. of death.
AHINADAB, ahin'-na-dab, liberal or noble b.
AHINOAM, ahin'-no-am, b. of grace.
AHIO, ahi'-o, brotherly.
AHIRA, ahi'-rah, brother of evil.
AHIRAM, ahi'-ram, b. of height.
AHISAMACH, ahis'-sa-mak, b. of support or aid.
AHISHAHAR, ahi'-sha-har, or b. of the dawn.
AHISHAR, ahi'-shar, b. of the singer, or of the upright.
AHITHOPHEL, ahit'-to-fel, b. of folly.
AHITUB, ahi'-tub, b. or friend of goodness.
AHLAB, ah'-lab, fatness, fertility.
AHLAI, ah'-lai, oh that!
AHOAH, aho'-ah, brotherhood.
AHOLAH, aho'-lah, she has her own tent.
AHOLIAB, aho'-li-ab, father's tent.
AHOLIBAH, aho'-li-bah, my tent is in her.
AHOLIBAMAH, aho-li-ba'-mah, tent of the high place.
AHUMAI, ahu'-mai, brother of (i.e., dweller near) water.
AHUZAM, ahuz'-am, their possession.
AHUZZATH, ahuz'-zath, possession.
AI, a'-i, a heap of ruins.
AIAH, ai'-ah, } hawk, falcon.
AJAH, a'-jah,
AIATH, ai'-ath, ruins.
AIJALON, ai'-ja-lon, } place of ga-
AJALON, ad'-ja-lon, } zelles.
AIN, an eye, a fountain.
AKKUB, ak'-kub, insidious.
AKRABBIM, ak-rab'-him, scorpions.
ALAMMELECH, al-lam'-me-lek, king's oak.
ALAMETH, al'-a-meth, } ^overing.
ALEMETH, al'-e-meth,
ALEXANDER, al-ex-an'-der, the helper of men.
ALEXANDRIA, al-ex-an'-dri-a, (the city named after Alexander).
ALIAH, a-li'-ah (see Alvah).
ALIAN, a-li'-an, tall, thick.
ALLON, al'-lon, an oak.
ALLON-BACHUTH, al-lon-bah'-kooth, o. of weeping.
ALMODAD, al-mo'-dad, extension (?)
ALMON, al'-mon, hidden

ALMON-DIBLATHAIM, al'-mon-dib-la-thay'-im, hiding of the twin cakes.
ALOTH, a'-loth, yielding milk (?)
ALPHA, al'-fah (the first letter of the Greek alphabet).
ALPHÆUS, al-feo'-us, learned, chief.
ALVAH, al'-vah, iniquity.
ALVAN, al'-van, tall, thick.
AMAD, a'-mad, eternal people.
AMAL, a'-mal, labour, sorrow.
AMALEK, am'-ma-lek (uncertain, probably derived from the preceding word).
AMAM, a'-mam, meeting-place.
AMANA, a-ma'-nah, or am'-a-nah, fixed, perennial.
AMARIAH, am-a-ri'-ah, whom Jehovah spoke of (i.e., promised).
AMASA, a-ma'-sah, burden.
AMASAI, am-as'-ai, } burden-
AMASHAI, am-ash'-ai, } some.
AMAZIAH, am-a-zi'-ah, whom Jehovah bears.
AMI, a'-my (probably a form of Amm).
AMITTAI, amit'-tai, true.
AMMAH, am'-mah, beginning, head.
AMMI, am'-my, my people.
AMMIEL, am'-mi-el, people of God.
AMMIHUD, am-mi'-hud, p. of Judah.
AMMINADAB, am-min'-a-dab, p. of the prince.
AMMISHADDAI, am-my-shad'-dai, p. of the Almighty.
AMMIZABAD, am-miz'-a-bad, p. of the giver (i.e., Jehovah).
AMMON, am'-mon, son of my p.
AMNON, am'-non, faithful.
AMOK, a'-mok, deep.
AMON, a'-mon, foster-child.
AMORITE, am'-mo-rite, mountaineer.
AMOS, a'-mos, burden.
AMOZ, a'-moz, strong.
AMPHIPOLIS, am-fip'-po-lis, around the city.
AMPLIAS, am'-pli-as, large, extensive, making more.
AMRAM, am'-ram, people of the highest (i.e., God).
AMRAPHEL, am'-ra-fel, guardian of the gods (?)
AMZI, am'-zy, strong.
ANAB, a'-nab, place of clusters (of grapes).
ANAH, a'-nah, answering.
ANAHARATH, an-na-hah'-rath, snorting, or gorge (?)

ANAIAH, an-nai'-yah, whom Jehovah has answered.

ANAK, a'-nak, long-necked, giant.

ANAMMELECH, an-nam'-me-lek, image of the king, or, shepherd and flock (?)

ANAN, a'-nan, a cloud.

ANANI, an-a'-ny
ANANIAH, an-na-ni'-ah, } whom Jehovah covers (i. e., guards).

ANANIAS, an-na-ni'-as (see HANANIAH).

ANATH, a'-nath, an answer (to prayer).

ANATHOTH, an'-na-thoth, answers (to prayers).

ANDREW, an'-droo, a strong man, manly.

ANDRONICUS, an-dro-ni'-kus, or an-dron'-i-kus, a man excelling others, a victorious man.

ANEM, a'-nem, two fountains.

ANER, a'-ner, a young man.

ANIAM, a-ni'-am, sorrow of the people.

ANIM, a'-nim, fountains.

ANNA, an'-na, gracious.

ANNAS, an'-nas (see HANANIAH).

ANTIOCH, an'-ti-ok, withstanding (?)

ANTIPAS, an'-ti-pas (contraction of Antipater), for or like the father.

ANTIPATRIS, an-ti-pat'-tris (from the foregoing).

ANTOTHIJAH, an-to-thi'-jah, prayers answered by Jehovah.

ANUB, a'-nub, bound together.

APELLES, ap-pel'-lees, separated.

APHARSACHITES, af-far'-sa-kites.

APHEK, a'-fek,
APHEKAH, a-fe'-kah, } strength, fortress, fortified city (?) watercress.

APHIAH, af-fi'-ah, rekindled, refreshed.

APHRAH, af'-rah, dust.

APHSES, af'-sees, dispersion.

APOLLONIA, ap-pol-lo'-ni-a (named after the god Apollo.

APOLLOS, ap-pol'-los, one that destroys.

APOLLYON, ap-pol'-yon, one that exterminates.

APPAIM, ap'-pay-im, the nostrils.

APPHIA, ap'-fi-a, bringing forth, fruitful.

APPII-FORUM, ap'-py-i-fo'-rum, forum, or market-place of Appius.

AQUILA, ak'-wy-lah, an eagle.

AR, city.

ARA, a'-ra, lion.

ARAB, a'-rab, ambush, lying in wait.

ARABAH, ar'-a-bah,
ARABIA, ar-ra'-bya, } a sterile region.

ARAD, a'-rad, wild ass.

ARAH, a'-rah, wandering.

ARAM, a'-ram, height, high region.

ARAN, a'-ran, wild goat.

ARARAT, ar'-ra-rat, holy ground.

ARAUNAH, ar-raw'-nah, ark (?) an ash or pine tree (?)

ARBA, ar'-bah, hero of Baal.

ARCHELAUS, ar-ke-la'-us, prince of the people.

ARCHEVITES, ar'-ke-vites, (the men of Erech, q. v.)

ARCHI, ar'-ky (also from Erech).

ARCHIPPUS, ar-kip'-pus, master of the horse.

ARCTURUS, ark-tu'-rus, an ark, a bier (?)

ARD, fugitive (?)

ARDON, ar'-don, fugitive.

ARELI, are'-ly, sprung from a hero, son of a hero.

AREOPAGUS, a-re-op'-pa-gus, hill of Mars.

ARETAS, a'-re-tas, one that is virtuous, pleasant.

ARGOB, ar'-gob, a heap of stones.

ARIDAI, a-rid'-dai,
ARIDATHA, a-rid'-da-thah, } strong.

ARIEH, a'-ri-eh, lion.

ARIEL, a'-ri-el, lion of God.

ARIMATHÆA, ar-ry-ma-thee'-ya, the heights.

ARIOCH, a'-ri-yok, }
ARISAI, ar-ris'-sai, } lion-like.

ARISTARCHUS, ar-ris-tar'-kus, best excellent chief.

ARISTOBULUS, ar-ris-to-bu'-lus, a good counsellor, the best advice.

ARKITE, ark'-ite, fugitive.

ARMAGEDDON, ar-ma-ged'-don, height of Megiddo.

ARMENIA, ar-me'-nya,

ARMONI, ar-mo'-ny, imperial.

ARNAN, ar'-nan, nimble.

ARNON, ar'-non, noisy.

AROD, a'-rod,
ARODI, a'-rod-dy, } wild ass.

AROER, ar'-ro-er, ruins (?)

ARPAD, ar'-pad,
ARPHAD, ar'-fad, } support.

ARPHAXAD, ar-fax'-ad,

ARTAXERXES, ar-tax-erx'-ees, powerful warrior.
ARTEMAS, ar'-te-mas, whole, sound, without fault.
ARUBOTH, ar'-ru-both, windows.
ARUMAH, a-roo'-mah, elevated.
ARVAD, ar'-vad, a wandering, place of fugitives.
ARZA, ar'-za, earth.
ASA, a'-sah, physician.
ASAHEL, as'-sa-hel, } whom God
ASAIAH, as-sai'-yah, } made (i.e., constituted, appointed).
ASAPH, a'-saf, collector.
ASAREEL, as-sar'-re-el, whom God has bound.
ASARELAH, as-sar-e'-lah, upright to God.
ASENATH, as'-e-nath, she who is of Neith (i.e., Minerva of the Egyptians).
ASHAN, a'-shan, smoke.
ASHBEL, ash'-bel, determination of God.
ASHDOD, ash'-dod, a fortified place, a castle.
ASHDOTH-PISGAH, ash'-doth-piz'-gah, outpourings of Pisgah.
ASHER, ash'-er, fortunate, happy.
ASHERAH, ash-e'-rah, fortune, happiness.
ASHIMA, ash'-shy-ma, a goat with short hair.
ASHKELON, ash'-ke-lon, } migration.
ASKELON, as'-ke-lon, }
ASHKENAZ, ash'-ke-naz,
ASHNAH, ash'-nah, strong, mighty.
ASHPENAZ, ash'-pe-naz, horse's nose.
ASHTAROTH, ash'-ta-roth, statues of Ashtoreth.
ASHTORETH, ash'-to-reth, star, specially the planet Venus, the goddess of love and fortune.
ASIA, a'-shya.
ASIEL, a'-si-el, created by God.
ASNAH, as'-nah, storehouse, bramble.
ASNAPPER, as-nap'-per, leader of an army (?)
ASPATHA, as'-pa-thah, a horse, bullock.
ASRIEL, as'-ri-el, the vow of God.
ASSHUR, ash'-ur, blackness.
ASSIR, as'-seer, captive.
ASSOS, as'-sos,
ASSYRIA, as-syr'-rya (named from Asshur).
ASTAROTH, as'-ta-roth, } (see ASH-
ASTARTE, as-tar'-tee, } TORETH.)
ASUPPIM, as-sup'-pim, collections.

ASYNCRITUS, as-sin'-kry-tus, incomparable.
ATAD, a'-tad, buckthorn.
ATARAH, at'-ta-rah, a crown.
ATAROTH, at'-ta-roth, } crowns.
ATROTH, at'-roth, }
ATER, a'-ter, bound, shut up.
ATHACH, a'-thak, lodging-place.
ATHAIAH, athai'-yah, whom Jehovah made.
ATHALIAH, ath-a-li'-ah, whom Jehovah has afflicted.
ATHLAI, ath'-lai.
ATHENS, ath'-ens.
ATTAI, at'-tai, opportune.
ATTALIA, at-ta-li'-a.
AUGUSTUS, aw-gus'-tus, increasing, majestic.
AVEN, a'-ven, nothingness.
AVIM, av'-vim, } ruins.
AVITH, av'-vith, }
AZAL, a'-zal, noble, root, declivity.
AZALIAH, a-za-li'-ah, whom Jehovah has reserved.
AZANIAH, az-a-ni'-ah, whom Jehovah hears.
AZARAEL, az-a'-ra-el, } whom God
AZAREEL, az-a'-re-el, } helps.
AZARIAH, az-a-ri'-ah, whom Jehovah aids.
AZAZ, a'-zaz, strong.
AZAZIAH, az-a-zi'-ah, whom Jehovah strengthened.
AZBUK, az'-buk, altogether desolated.
AZEKAH, az-e'-kah, a field dug over, broken up.
AZEL, a'-zel, noble.
AZEM, a'-zem, strength, bone.
AZGAD, az'-gad, strong in fortune.
AZIEL, az'-zi-el, whom God consoles.
AZIZA, az-zi'-zah, strong.
AZMAVETH, az-ma'-veth, strong to death.
AZMON, az'-mon, robust.
AZNOTH-TABOR, az'-noth-ta'-bor, ears (i.e., summits) of Tabor.
AZOR, a'-zor, }
AZUR, a'-zur, } helper.
AZZUR, az'-zur, }
AZOTH, or AZOTUS, { az'-zoth, az-zo'-tus, } (the Greek form of ASHDOD, q.v.).
AZRIEL, az'-ri-el, whom God helps.
AZRIKAM, az-ri'-kam, help against an enemy.
AZUBAH, a-zu'-bah, forsaken.

AZZAH, az'-zah, the strong, fortified.

AZZAN, az'-zan, very strong.

BAAL, ba'-al, lord, master, possessor, owner.

BAALAH, ba'-a-lah,
BAALATH, ba'-a-lath, } mistress.

BAALATH-BEER, ba'-a-lath-be'-er, having a well.

BAAL-BERITH, ba'-al-be-reeth', covenant lord.

BAAL-GAD, ba'-al-gad, lord of fortune.

BAAL-HAMON, ba'-al-ha'-mon, place of a multitude.

BAAL-HANAN, ba'-al-ha'-nan, lord of benignity.

BAAL-HAZOR, ba'-al-ha'-zor, having a village.

BAAL-HERMON, ba'-al-her'-mon, place of Hermon.

BAALI, ba'-a-ly, my lord.

BAALIM, ba'-a-lim, lords.

BAALIS, ba'-a-lis, son of exultation.

BAAL-MEON, ba'-al-me'-on, place of habitation.

BAAL-PEOR, ba'-al-pe'-or, lord of the opening.

BAAL-PERAZIM, ba'-al-pe-ra'-zim, place of breaches.

BAAL-SHALISHA, ba'-al-sha'-li-shah, lord (or place) of shalisha.

BAAL-TAMAR, ba'-al-ta'-mar, place of palm-trees.

BAAL-ZEBUB, ba-al'-ze-bub, lord of the fly.

BAAL-ZEPHON, ba'-al-ze'-phon, place of Typhon, or sacred to Typhon.

BAANA, ba'-a-nah,
BAANAH, } son of affliction.

BAARA, ba'-a-rah, foolish.

BAASEIAH, ba-a-si'-ah, work of Jehovah.

BAASHA, ba'-a-sha, wickedness.

BABEL, ba'-bel,
BABYLON, bab'-by-lon, } confusion.

BACA, ba'-kah, weeping.

BAHURIM, ba-hu'-rim, young men.

BAJITH, ba'-jith (same as Beth), house.

BAKBAKKAR, bak-bak'-kar, wasting of the mountain.

BAKBUKIAH, bak-buk-i'-ah, emptying (i. e., wasting) of Jehovah.

BALAAM, ba'-lam, foreigner.

BALADAN, bal'-la-dan, whose Lord is Bel.

BALAH, ba'-lah, bushfulness (?)

BALAK, ba'-lak, empty, void.

BAMAH, ba'-mah, high place.

BAMOTH, ba'-moth, high places

BAMOTH-BAAL, ba'-moth-ba'-al, h. p. of Baal.

BANI, ba'-ny, built.

BARABBAS, ba-rab'-bas, son of Abba, or of shame.

BARACHEL, bar'-ra-kel, whom God blessed.

BARACHIAH, bar-ra-ki'-ah,
BARACHIAS, bar-ra-ki'-as, } whom Jehovah blesses.

BARAK, ba'-rak, thunderbolt, lightning.

BARHUMITE, bar-hu'-mite,
BAHARUMITE, ba-har'-u-mite, } an inhabitant of Bahurim, q. v.

BARIAH, ba-ri'-ah, a fugitive.

BAR-JESUS, bar-je'-sus, son of Jesus, or Joshua.

BAR-JONA, bar-jo'-na, s. of Jonah.

BARKOS, bar'-kos, painter.

BARNABAS, bar'-na-bas, son of comfort.

BARSABAS, bar'-sa-bas, s. of Saba.

BARTHOLOMEW, bar-thol'-o-mew, s. of Talmai.

BARTIMÆUS, bar-ty-mee'-us, s. of Timæus.

BARUCH, ba'-rook, blessed.

BARZILLAI, bar-zil'-lai, of iron.

BASHAN, ba'-shan, soft, sandy soil.

BASHAN-HAVOTH-JAIR, ba'-shan-hav'-voth-jay'-yir, B. of the villages of Jair.

BASHEMATH, bash'-e-math, sweet smelling.

BATHRABBIM, bath-rab'-bim, daughter of many.

BATH-SHEBA, bath'-she-bah, d. of the oath.

BATH-SHUA, bath'-shu-ah, d. of wealth.

BAVAI, bav'-vai, son of wishing (?)

BAZLITH, baz'-lith, a making naked.

BEALIAH, be-a-li'-ah, whom Jehovah rules.

BEALOTH, be'-a-loth, citizens (?) See BAALATH.

BEBAI, be'-bai, father, paternal.

BECHER, be'-ker, a young camel, or firstborn.

BECHORATH, be-kor'-ath, offspring of the first birth.

BEDAD, be'-dad, separation, part.

BEDAN, be'-dan, servile.

BEDEIAH, be-di'-yah, in the protection of Jehovah.

BEELIADA, be-el-i'-a-dah, whom the Lord has known.
BEELZEBUB, be-el'-ze-bub. (See BAAL-ZEBUB.)
BEER, be'-er,
BEERA, be-e'-rah, a well.
BEERAH,
BEER-ELIM, be-er-e'-lim, w. of heroes.
BEERI, be-e'-ry, man of the w.
BEER-LAHAI-ROI, be-er'-la-hah'-y-ro'-y, w. of seeing (God) and living.
BEEROTH, be-e'-roth, wells.
BEER-SHEBA, be-er'-she-bah, well of the oath.
BEESHTERAH, be-esh'-te-rah, house or temple of Astarte.
BEHEMOTH, be-he'-moth (but more commonly pronounced in English, be'-he-moth), great beast, or perhaps water-ox.
BEKAH, be'-kah, part, half.
BEL, bel. (See BAAL.)
BELA, be'-lah, destruction.
BELAH,
BELIAL, be'-li-al, worthless.
BELSHAZZAR, bel-shaz'-zar,
BELTESHAZZAR, bel-te-shaz'-zar, Bel's prince (i.e., prince whom Bel favours).
BEN, ben, son.
BENAIAH, be-nai'-yah, whom Jehovah has built.
BEN-AMMI, ben-am'-my, son of my own kindred.
BENE-BERAK, ben-e'-be-rak, sons of Barak (or of lightning).
BENE-JAAKAN, ben-e-ja'-a-kan, s. of Jordan.
BEN-HADAD, ben-ha'-dad, s. of Hadad.
BEN-HAIL, ben-hah'-il, s. of the host (i.e., warrior).
BEN-HANAN, ben-ha'-nan, s. of one who is gracious.
BENINU, ben-ee'-noo, our s.
BENJAMIN, ben'-ja-min, s. of the right hand.
BENO, ben'-o, his s.
BEN-ONI, ben-o'-ny, s. of my sorrow.
BEN-ZOHETH, ben-zo'-heth, s. of Zoheth.
BEON, be'-on (contracted from Baal-meon, q. v.).
PEOR, be'-or, torch, lamp.
BERA, be'-ra, son of evil (?)
BERACHAH, ber-a'-kah, blessing.
BERACHIAH, ber-a-ki'-ah, whom
BERECHIAH, ber-e-ki'-ah, Jehovah hath blessed.

BERAIAH, be-rai'-yah, whom Jehovah created.
BEREA, be-re'-a.
BERED, be'-red, hail.
BERI, be'-ry. (See BEERI.)
BERIAH, be-ri'-ah, son of evil (?) a gift (?)
BERIITES, be-ri'-ites, descendants of Beriah.
BERITH, be'-rith, a covenant.
BERNICE, ber-ni'-see, bringer of victory.
BERODACH-BALADAN, ber'-o-dak-bal'-a-dan, Berodach, worshipper of Bel.
BEROTHAH, ber'-o-thah, my wells.
BEROTHAI, ber'-o-thai,
BESAI, be'-sai, sword, or victory (?)
BESODEIAH, be-so-di'-ah, in the secret of Jehovah.
BESOR, be'-sor, cold, to be cold, as water.
BETAH, be'-tah, confidence.
BETEN, be'-ten, valley.
BETHABARA, beth-ab'-a-rah, house of passage.
BETH-ANATH, beth'-a-nath, h. of
BETH-ANOTH, beth'-a-noth, response, or echo.
BETHANY, beth'-a-ny, h. of dates.
BETH-ARABAH, beth-ar'-a-bah, h. of the desert.
BETH-ARAM, beth-a'-ram, h. of the height.
BETH-ARBEL, beth-ar'-bel, h. of the ambush o. God.
BETH-AVEN, beth-a'-ven, h. of vanity (i.e., of idols).
BETH-AZMAVETH, beth-az-ma'-veth, h. strong as death.
BETH-BAAL-MEON, beth'-ba-al-me'-on, h. of Baal-meon.
BETHBARAH, beth'-ba-rah. (See BETHABARA.)
BETH-BIREI, beth-bir'-i, h. of my creation.
BETH-CAR, beth'-kar, h. of pasture.
BETH-DAGON, beth-da'-gon, h. of Dagon.
BETH-DIBLATHAIM, beth-dib-la-thay'-im, h. of the two cakes.
BETH-EL, beth'-el, h. of God.
BETH-EMEK, beth-e'-mek, h. of the valley.
BETHER, be'-ther, separation.
BETHESDA, beth-es'-dah, house of mercy.
BETH-EZEL, beth-e'-zel, h. of firm root (i.e., of fixed dwelling).

BETH-GADER, beth-ga'-der, *h.* of the wall.

BETH-GAMUL, beth-ga'-mul, *h.* of the weaned.

BETH-HACCEREM, beth-hak'-ker-em, *h.* of the vineyard.

BETH-HAGGAN, beth-hag'-gan, the garden-*h.*

BETH-HARAN, beth-ha'-ran, *h.* of the height.

ETH-HOGLAH, beth-hog'-lah, *h.* of the partridge.

ETH-HORON, beth-ho'-ron, *h.* of the hollow.

BETH-JESHIMOTH, beth-jesh'-i-moth, *h.* of the deserts.

BETH-LEBAOTH, beth-leb'-a-oth, *h.* of lionesses.

BETH-LEHEM, beth'-le-hem, *h.* of bread.

BETH-LEHEM-EPHRATAH, beth'-le-hem-ef'-ra-tah, B. the fruitful (?)

BETH-LEHEM-JUDAH, beth'-le-hem-ju'-dah, B. of Judah.

BETH-MAACHAH, beth-ma'-a-kah, house of Maachah.

BETH-MARCABOTH, beth-mar'-ca-both, *h.* of chariots.

BETH-MEON, beth-me'-on, *h.* of habitation.

BETH-NIMRAH, beth-nim'-rah, *h.* of limpid and sweet water.

BETH-PALET, beth-pa'-let, *h.* of escape, or of Pelet.

BETH-PAZZEZ, beth-paz'-zez, *h.* of dispersion.

BETH-PEOR, beth-pe'-or, temple of (Baal) Peor.

BETHPHAGE, beth-fa'-jee, house of unripe figs.

BETH-PHALET, beth-fa'-let. (See BETH-PALET.)

BETH-RAPHA, beth-ra'-fah, house of the giant.

BETH-REHOB, beth-re'-hob, *h.* or region of breadth.

BETHSAIDA, beth-sa'-i-da, *h.* of fishing.

BETH-SHAN, beth'-shan, } *h.* of
BETH-SHEAN, beth-she'-an, } rest.

BETH-SHEMESH, beth'-she-mesh, *h.* of the sun.

BETH-SHITTAH, beth-shit'-tah, *h.* of acacias.

BETH-TAPPUAH, beth-tap'-pu-ah, *h.* of apples or citrons.

BETHUEL, be-thu'-el, man of God.

BETHUL, be-thewl', abode of God, tarrying of God.

BETH-ZUR, beth'-zur, house of the rock.

BETONIM, be-to'-nim, pistachio nuts.

PEULAH, be-ew'-lah, married.

BEZAI, be'-zai, victory.

BEZALEEL, be-zal'-e-el, in the shadow (*i. e.*, the protection) of God.

BEZEK, be'-zek, lightning.

BEZER, be'-zer, ore of precious metal.

BICHRI, bik'-ri, juvenile.

BIDKAR, bid'-kar, son of piercing through.

BIGTHA, big'-thah,
BIGTHAN, big'-than, } gift of
BIGTHANA, big'-tha-nah, } fortune.

BIGVAI, big'-vai, husbandman (?) happy (?)

BILDAD, bil'-dad, son of contention.

BILEAM, bil'-e-am, foreign.

BILGAH, bil'-gah, } cheerfulness.
BILGAI, bil'-gai, }

BILHAH, bil'-hah, modesty.

BILHAN, bil'-han, modest.

BILSHAN, bil'-shan, son of tongue (*i. e.*, eloquent).

BIMHAL, bim'-hal, son of circumcision.

BINEA, bin'-e-ah, a gushing forth.

BINNUI, bin'-nu-i, building.

BIRSHA, bir'-sha, son of wickedness.

BIRZAVITH, bir'-za-vith, apertures, wounds (?) well of olives (?)

BISHLAM, bish'-lam, son of peace.

BITHIAH, bith-i'-ah, daughter (*i. e.*, worshipper) of Jehovah.

BITHRON, bith'-ron, section.

BITHYNIA, bi-thinn'-ya.

BIZJOTHIAH, biz-joth'-i-ah, } contempt of Jehovah.
BIZJOTHJAH, biz-joth'-jah, }

BIZTHA, biz'-tha, eunuch.

BLASTUS, blas'-tus, one who sprouts, gum.

BOANERGES, bo-an-er'-jes, sons of thunder.

BOAZ, bo'-az, } fleetness.
BOOZ, bo'-oz, }

BOCHERU, bok'-e-roo, he is firstborn.

BOCHIM, bo'-kim, weepers.

BOHAN, bo'-han, thumb.

BOSCATH, bos'-kath, stony, elevated ground.

BOSOR, bo'-sor (same as Beor, q. v.).

BOZEZ, bo'-zez, shining.

BOZRAH, boz'-rah, a fold, sheepfold

BUKKI, buk'-ki, wasting.

BUKKIAH, buk-ki'-ah, w. of Jehovah.

BUNAH, bew'-na, prudence.

BUNNI, bun'-ni, built.

BUZ, buzz, despised, or contemned.

BUZI, bew'-zi, descended from Buz.

CAB, kab, hollow.

CABBON, kab'-bon, bond, cake.

CABUL, ka'-bul, as nothing.

CÆSAR, see'-zar, a cut or gash.

CAIAPHAS, kai'-ya-fas, depression.

CAIN, kane, } a possession,
CAINAN, kai'-nan, } possessed, or acquired.

CALAH, kah'-lah, old age.

CALCOL, kal'-kol, sustenance.

CALEB, ka'-leb, a dog.

CALEB-EPHRATAH, ka'-leb-ef'-ra-tah, C. the fruitful.

CALNEH, kal'-nay, } fortified and
CALNO, kal'-no, } willing.

CALVARY, kal'-va-ry, skull.

CAMON, ka'-mon, abounding in stalks.

CANA, ka'-nah, reedy.

CANAAN, ka'-nan, depressed, low region, merchant.

CANDACE, kan-da'-see, who possesses, sovereign of slaves (?)

CANNEH, kan'-nay, plant or shoot.

CAPERNAUM, ka-per'-na-um, city of consolation (?)

CAPHTOR, kaf'-tor, chaplet, knop (?)

CAPHTORIM, kaf'-to-rim, inhabitants of Caphtor.

CAPPADOCIA, kap-pa-do'-shya.

CARCAS, kar'-kas, eagle (?) severe.

CARCHEMISH, kar'-ke-mish, fortress of Chemosh.

CAREAH, ka-re'-ah, bald.

CARMEL, kar'-mel, the mountain of the garden, park.

CARMI, kar'-my, a vinedresser.

CARPUS, kar'-pus, fruit, or fruitful.

CARSHENA, kar'-she-nah, spoiling of war.

CASIPHIA, ka-sif'-i-a, silver (?)

CASLEU, kas'-lew, languid.

CASLUHIM, kas'-lu-him, fortified.

CASTOR, kas'-tor.

CENCHREA, sen'-kre-a, millet, small pulse.

CEPHAS, see'-fas, a rock, or stone.

CESAREA, see-zar-e'-a, named after (Augustus) Cæsar.

CESAREA-PHILIPPI, see-zar-e'-a-fil-lip'-pi, named after Philip (the tetrarch).

CHALCOL, kal'-kol, sustenance.

CHALDEA, kal-de'-a.

CHARASHIM, ka-ra'-shim, craftsmen.

CHARRAN, kar'-ran. (See HARAN.)

CHEBAR, ke'-bar, length.

CHEDORLAOMER, ked-dor-la'-o-mer, a handful of sheaves.

CHELAL, ke'-lal, completion.

CHELLUH, kel'-lew, the state or condition of a bride, completed.

CHELUB, ke'-lub, basket.

CHELUBAI, kel'-lu-bai (same as Caleb, q. v.).

CHEMARIMS, ke-ma'-rims, in black (attire).

CHEMOSH, ke'-mosh, subduer, conqueror, tamer.

CHENAANAH, ke-na'-a-nah, merchant.

CHENANI, ke-na'-ny, protector.

CHENANIAH, ken-a-ni'-ah, whom Jehovah hath set.

CHEPHAR-HAAMMONAI, ke'-far-ha-am'-mo-nai, village of the Ammonites.

CHEPHIRAH, ke-fi'-rah, village.

CHERAN, ke'-ran, a harp, lyre.

CHERETHIMS, ker'-eth-ims, Cretans (?)

CHERETHITES, ker'-eth-ites, executioners, runners.

CHERITH, ke'-rith, } separation.
CHERISH, ke'-rish, }

CHERUB, ke'-rub, } a herald (?)
CHERUB, tsher'-ub, } strong (?)

CHERUBIM, tsher'-u-bim (plural of cherub).

CHESALON, kes'-a-lon, confidence, hope.

CHESED, ke'-sed, gain.

CHESIL, ke'-sil, a fool, ungodly.

CHESULLOTH, ke-sul'-loth, confidences.

CHEZIB, ke'-zib, false.

CHIDON, ki'-don, dart, javelin.

CHILEAB, kil'-le-ab, whom the father (i. e., Creator) has perfected.

CHILION, kil'-le-on, wasting away.

CHILMAD, kil'-mad.

CHIMHAM, kim'-ham, languishing, longing.

CHINNERETH, kin'-ne-reth, } a lyre.
CHINNEROTH, kin'-ne-roth, }

CHIOS, ki'-os, open, or opening.

CHISLEU, kis'-lew, languid.

CHISLON, kis'-lon, confidence, hope.

CHISLOTH-TABOR, kis'-loth-ta-bor, flanks of Tabor.
CHITTIM, kit'-tim, men of Cyprus.
CHIUN, ki'-youn, statue, image.
CHLOE, klo'-ee, green herb.
CHORASHAN, ko-ra'-shan, smoking furnace.
CHORAZIN } ko-ra'-zin, { the secrets
CHORASIN }   { or mystery.
CHOZEBA, ko-ze'-ba, lying.
CHRIST, the anointed (equivalent to MESSIAH).
CHRONICLES, kron'-i-kls, records of history.
CHUB, kub, the people of Nubia (?)
CHUN, kun, establishment, place (?)
CHUSHAN-RISHATHAIM, ku'-shan-rish-a-thay'-im, most malicious, or wicked Cushite.
CHUZA, kew'-za, seer.
CILICIA, si-lish'-ya.
CINNERETH, kin'-ne-reth. (See CHINNEROTH.)
CLAUDA, klaw'-da.
CLAUDIA, klaw'-dya.
CLAUDIUS, klaw'-di-us.
CLEMENT, klem'-ent, mild, good, modest.
CLEOPAS, kle'-o-pas, } learned, the
CLEOPHAS, kle'-o-fas, } whole glory.
CNIDUS, ni'-dus.
COL-HOZEH, kol-ho'-zeh, all-seeing.
COLOSSE, ko-los'-see.
COLOSSIANS, ko-los'-syans, people of Colosse.
CONIAH, ko-ni'-ah (contracted from JECONIAH, q. v.).
CONONIAH, kon-o-ni'-ah, whom Jehovah defends, has set up.
COOS, ko'-os.
COR, kor, a round vessel.
CORE, ko'-re. (See KORAH.)
CORINTH, kor'-inth.
CORINTHIANS, ko-rinth'-yans, inhabitants of Corinth.
CORNELIUS, kor-ne'-li-us, of a horn.
COS, kos.
COSAM, ko'-sam, diviner.
COZ, koz, horn.
COZBI, koz'-by, lying.
CRESCENS, kres'-sens, growing.
CRETE, kreet.
CRETIANS, kreet'-yans, inhabitants of Crete.
[...] -rua. curled.

CUSH, kush, }
CUSHAN, kush'-an, } black.
CUSHI, kush'-i, }
CUTH, kuth, } treasure-
CUTHA, ku'-thah, } house (?)
CUTHEANS, ku-the'-ans, inhabitants of Cuth.
CYPRUS, si'-prus.
CYRENE, si-re'-nee.
CYRENIUS, si-re'-ni-us, who governs.
CYRUS, si'-rus, the sun.

DABAREH, dab'-a-ray, } sheep-
DABERATH, dab'-e-rath, } walk.
DABBASHETH, dab'-bash-eth, hump of a camel.
DAGON, da'-gon, little fish.
DALAIAH, da-lai'-yah, whom Jehovah hath freed.
DALMANUTHA, dal-ma-nu'-tha.
DALMATIA, dal-may'-shya.
DALPHON, dal'-fon, swift.
DAMARIS, dam'-a-ris, a little woman.
DAMASCENES, dam-a-seens', people of Damascus.
DAMASCUS, da-mas'-kus, activity.
DAN, dan, judge.
DANJAAN, dan-ja'-an, woodland Dan.
DANIEL, dan'-yel, God's judge.
DANNAH, dan'-nah, low place.
DARA, da'-rah (probably contracted from the next word).
DARDA, dar'-dah, pearl of wisdom.
DARIUS, da-ri'-us, compeller (?)
DARKON, dar'-kon, scatterer.
DATHAN, da'-than, belonging to a fountain.
DAVID, da'-vid, beloved.
DEBIR, de'-ber, inner sanctuary.
DEBORAH, deb'-o-rah, bee.
DECAPOLIS, de-kap'-o-lis, ten cities.
DEDAN, de'-dan, lowland.
DEDANIM, de'-dan-im, inhabitants of Dedan.
DEHAVITES, de-ha'-vites, villagers.
DEKAR, de'-kar, piercing through.
DELAIAH, de-lai'-yah, whom Jehovah has freed.
DELILAH, de-li'-lah, feeble, pining with desire, weak, delicate.
DEMAS, do'-mas, of the people (or contracted from the next word).
DEMETRIUS, de-me'-tri-us, belonging to Ceres.
DERBE, der'-bee, juniper (?)
DEUEL, de-u'-el, invocation of God.

DEUTERONOMY, dew-ter-on'-o-my, a recapitulation of the law.

DIANA, di-an'-na, light-giving, perfect.

DIBLAIM, dib-lay'-im, } two
DIBLATHAIM, dib-la-thay'-im } cakes.

DIBLATH, dib'-lath (supposed to be the same as Riblah, q. v.).

DIBON, di'-bon, pining.

DIBON-GAD, di'-bon-gad, p. of Gad.

DIBRI, dib'-ry, eloquent.

DIDYMUS, did'-dy-mus, twin.

DIKLAH, dik'-lah, a palm tree.

DILEAN, dil'-e-an, cucumber field.

DIMNAH, dim'-nah, dunghill.

DIMON, di'-mon, } stillness.
DIMONAH, di-mo'-nah, }

DINAH, di'-nah, judged (i. e., acquitted), vindicated.

DINAITES, di'-na-ites, people of Dinah.

DINHABAH, din-ha'-bah, a lurking-place of robbers.

DIONYSIUS, di-o-nish'-yus, belonging to Dionysus, or Bacchus.

DIOTREPHES, di-ot'-re-fees, nourished by Jupiter.

DISHAN, di'-shan, antelope.

DIZAHAB, diz'-a-hab, a place abounding in gold.

DODAI, do'-dai, loving.

DODANIM, dod-a'-nim, leaders.

DODAVAH, dod-a'-vah, love of Jehovah.

DODO, do'-do, belonging to love.

DOEG, do'-eg, fearful.

DOPHKAH, dof'-kah, knocking.

DOR, dor, dwelling.

DORCAS, dor'-kas, the female of a roebuck.

DOTHAN, do'-than, two wells, or cisterns.

DRUSILLA, droo-sil'-la, dew-watered.

DUMAH, dew'-mah, silence.

DURAH, dew'-rah, circle.

EBAL, e'-bal, (1) void of leaves, (2) stony.

EBED, e'-bed, servant.

EBEDMELECH, e'-bed-me'-lek, servant of the king.

EBENEZER, eb-en-e'-zer, stone of help.

EBER, e'-ber, the region beyond, a passer over.

EBIASAPH, eb-bi'-a-saf, father of gathering.

EBRONAH, eb-ro'-nah, passage (of the sea).

ECCLESIASTES, ek-klee-zy-as'-teez, preacher.

ED, ed, witness.

EDAR, e'-dar, flock.

EDEN, e'-den, pleasantness.

EDER, e'-der, same as EDAR.

EDOM, e'-dom, red.

EDOMITES, e'-dom-ites, inhabitants of Idumea (or Edom).

EDREI, ed'-re-i, strong.

EGLAH, eg'-lah, heifer.

EGLAIM, eg-lay'-im, two pools.

EGLON, eg'-lon, pertaining to a calf.

EGYPT, e'-jipt.

EHI, e'-hi, my brother.

EHUD, e'-hud, joining together.

EKER, e'-ker, rooting up.

EKRON, ek'-ron, eradication.

ELADAH, el'-a-dah, whom God puts on.

ELAH, e'-lah, terebinth.

ELAM, e'-lam, age.

ELAMITES, e'-lam-ites, inhabitants of Elam (or Persia).

ELASAH, el'-a-sah, whom God made.

ELATH, e'-lath, trees, a grove (perhaps of palm trees).

EL-BETHEL, el-beth'-el, the God of Bethel.

ELDAAH, el'-da-ah, whom God called.

ELDAD, el'-dad, whom God loves.

ELEAD, el'-e-ad, whom God praises.

ELEALEH, el-e-a'-lay, whither God ascends.

ELEASAH, el-e'-a-sah, whom God made or created.

ELEAZAR, el-e-a'-zar, whom God aids.

EL-ELOHE-ISRAEL, el-el-o'-he-iz'-ra-el, God, the God of Israel.

ELEPH, e'-lef, ox.

ELHANAN, el-ha'-nan, whom God gave.

ELI, e'-li, going up, height, summit.

ELIAB, el-i'-ab, whose father is God.

ELIADA, } el-i'-a-dah, whom God
ELIADAH, } cares for.

ELIAH, el-i'-ah, my God is Jehovah.

ELIAHBA, el-i'-a-bah, whom God hides.

ELIAKIM, el-i'-a-kim, whom God has set.

ELIAM, el-i'-am, God's people.

ELIASAPH, el-i'-a-saf, whom God added.

ELIATHAH, el-i'-a-thah, to whom God comes.

ELIDAD, el-i'-dad, whom God loves.

ELIEL, el-i'-el, to whom God strength sc. gives.

ELIENAI, el-i-e'-nai, unto Jehovah my eyes (are turned).

ELIEZER, el-i-e'-zer, to whom God is help.

ELIHOREPH, el-i-ho'-ref, to whom God is the reward.

ELIHU, el-i'-hu, whose God is He.

ELIJAH, el-i'-jah, my God is Jehovah.

ELIKA, el-i'-kah, God of the congregation (?)

ELIM, e'-lim, trees.

ELIMELECH, el-im'-e-lek, to whom God is king.

ELIOENAI, el-i-o-e'-ni, unto Jehovah my eyes (are turned).

ELIPHAL, el-i'-fal, whom God judges.

ELIPHALET, el-i'-fal-et, }
ELIPHELET, el-i'-fel-et, } to whom God is salvation.

ELIPHAZ, el-i'-faz, to whom God is strength.

ELIPHELEH, el-i'-fel-eh, whom God distinguishes (i.e., makes distinguished).

ELISABETH, el-iz'-a-beth, the oath of God.

ELISHA, el-i'-sha, to whom God is salvation.

ELISHAH, el-i'-shah.

ELISHAMA, el-i'-sha-ma, whom God hears.

ELISHAPHAT, el-i'-sha-fat, whom God judges.

ELISHEBA, el-i'-she-ba, to whom God is the oath.

ELISHUA, el-i'-shu-ah, to whom God is salvation.

ELIUD, el-i'-hud, God of Judah.

ELIZAPHAN, el-i'-zaf-an, whom God protects.

ELIZUR, el-i'-zur, to whom God is a rock.

ELKANAH, el-ka'-nah, whom God created or possessed.

ELKOSHITE, el'-ko-shite, inhabitant of Elkosh.

ELLASAR, el'-la-sar, oak or heap of Assyria.

ELMODAM, el-mo'-dam, (same as ALMODAD, q. v.).

ELNAAM, el'-na-am, whose pleasure or joy God is.

ELNATHAN, el-na'-than, whom God gave.

ELON, e'-lon, oak.

ELONITES, e'-lon-ites, descendants of Elon.

ELON-BETH-HANAN, e'-lon-beth'-ha-nan, oak of the house of grace.

ELOTH, e'-loth, (same as ELATH, q. v.).

ELPAAL, el'-pa-al, to whom God is the reward.

ELPALET, el'-pa-let, to whom God is salvation.

ELPARAN, el'-pa-ran, oak of Paran.

ELTEKEH, el'-te-keh, to which God is fear (or object of fear).

ELTEKON, el'-te-kon, to which God is the foundation.

ELTOLAD, el'-to-lad, whose race or posterity is from God.

ELUZAI, el'-u-zai, God is my praises (i.e., my praises are directed to God).

ELYMAS, el'-y-mas, a corrupter, or sorcerer.

ELZABAD, el'-za-bad, whom God gave.

ELZAPHAN, el'-za-fan, whom God protects.

EMIMS, e'-mims, terrible men.

EMMANUEL, em-man'-u-el, God with us.

EMMAUS, em-ma'-us, hot springs.

EMMOR, em'-mor, (same as HAMOR, q. v.).

ENAM, e'-nam, two fountains.

ENAN, e'-nan, having eyes.

ENDOR, en'-dor, fountain of habitation.

ENEGLAIM, en-eg-la'-im, f. of two calves, or two pools.

ENGANNIM, en-gan'-nim, f. of gardens.

ENGEDI, en'-ge-di, f. of the kid.

ENHADDAH, en-had'-dah, f. of sharpness, i. e., swift.

ENHAKKORE, en-hak-ko'-ree, f. of the crier.

ENHAZOR, en-ha'-zor, f. of the village.

EN-MISHPAT, en-mish'-pat, f. of judgment.

ENOCH, e'-nok, initiated, or initiating.

ENON, e'non. (See ÆNON.)

ENOS, e'-nos, man.

ENRIMMON, en-rim'-mon, fountain of the pomegranate.

EN-ROGEL, en-ro'-gel, f. of the spy, or fuller's f.

ENSHEMESH, en-she'-mesh, f. of the sun.

ENTAPPUAH, en-tap'-pu-ah, f. of the apple tree.

EPAPHRAS, ep'-a-fras, (contracted from the next word).

EPAPHRODITUS, e-paf-ro-di'-tus, agreeable, handsome.

EPENETUS, e-pe′-ne-tus, laudable.
EPHAH, e′-fah, darkness.
EPHAI, e′-fai, wearied out, languishing.
EPHER, e′-fer, calf, young animal.
EPHES-DAMMIM, e′-fez-dam′-mim, sation of blood.
EPHESUS, ef′-fe-sus.
EPHESIANS, ef-fe′-zhi-ans, inhabitants of Ephesus.
EPHLAL, ef′-lal, judgment.
EPHOD, e′-fod, to gird on, put on.
EPHPHATHA, ef′-fa-thah, be opened.
EPHRAIM, ef′-ra-im, double land, twin land.
EPHRAIMITES, ef′-ra-im-ites, inhabitants of Ephraim.
EPHRATAH, ef′-ra-tah, land, region (?) or fruitful (?)
EPHRATHITES, ef′-rath-ites, inhabitants of Ephrath.
EPHRON, ef′-ron, of or belonging to a calf.
EPICUREANS, ep-i-ku-re′-ans, followers of Epicurus.
ER, err,
ERAN, e′-ran, } watcher, watchful.
ERANITES, e′-ran-ites, posterity of Eran.
ERASTUS, e-ras′-tus, lovely, amiable.
ERECH, e′-rek, length.
ERI, e′-ri, guarding (i. e., worshipping) Jehovah.
ERITES, e′-rites, inhabitants of Eri.
ESAR-HADDON, e′-sar-had′-don, gift of fire.
ESAU, e′-saw, hairy, rough.
ESEK, e′-sek, strife.
ESH-BAAL, esh′-ba-al, man or fire of Baal.
ESHBAN, esh′-ban, reason.
ESHCOL, esh′-kol, cluster.
ESHEAN, esh′-e-an, prop, support.
ESHEK, e′-shek, oppression.
ESHTAOL, esh′-ta-ol, petition, request.
ESHTEMOA, esh-tem-o′-ah, } obedience.
ESHTEMOTH, esh′-te-moth, }
ESHTON, esh′-ton, uxorious, womanly.
ESLI, es′-li, whom Jehovah reserved (?)
ESROM, es′-rom, (same as HEZRON, q. v.).
ESTHER, es′-ter, star, fortune, felicity.
ETAM, e′-tam, a place of ravenous creatures.

ETHAM, e′-tham, boundary of the sea (?)
ETHAN, e′-than, a wise man, firmness.
ETHBAAL, eth-ba′-al, living with Baal (i. e., enjoying the favour and help of Baal).
ETHER, e′-ther, plenty, abundance.
ETHIOPIA, e′-thi-op-ya, (region of) burnt faces.
ETHNAN, eth′-nan, a gift.
ETHNI, eth′-ni, bountiful, munificent.
EUBULUS, eu-bu′-lus, prudent, wise, good counsellor.
EUNICE, eu-ni′-see, good victory.
EUODIAS, eu-o′-di-as, sweet favour.
EUPHRATES, cu-fra′-tes, sweet water.
EUROCLYDON, eu-rok′-ly-don.
EUTYCHUS, eu′-ty-kus, fortunate.
EVE, eve, life.
EVI, e′-vi, desire, habitation.
EVIL-MERODACH, e′-vil-mer′-o-dak, the fool or worshipper of Merodach.
EXODUS, ex′-o-dus, going out, departure.
EZAR, e′-zar, treasure.
EZBAI, ez′-bai, hairy.
EZBON, ez′-bon, a worker.
EZEKIAS, ez-e-ki′-as. (See HEZEKIAH.)
EZEKIEL, ez-e′-ki-el, whom God will strengthen.
EZEL, e′-zel, departure.
EZEM, e′-zem, true strength.
EZER, e′-zer, help.
EZION-GEBER, e′-zi-on-ge′-ber, the back-bone of a giant.
EZNITE, ez′-nite.
EZRA, ez′-rah, help.
EZRAHITE, ez′-ra-hite, a descendant of Ezra, or Zerah.
EZRI, ez′-ri, ready to help, the help of Jehovah.
EZRON, ez′-ron. (See HEZRON.)

FELIX, fe′-lix, happy.
FESTUS, fes′-tus, joyful.
FORTUNATUS, for-tu-na′-tus, prosperous.

GAAL, ga′-al, loathing.
GAASH, ga′-ash, shaking, earthquake.
GABA, ga′-bah, hill.
GABBAI, gab′-bai, an exactor of tribute.
GABBATHA, gab′-ba-tha, platform.
GABRIEL, ga′-bri-el, man of God.

GAD, gad, a troop, good fortune.

GADARA, gad'-a-rah.

GADARENES, gad-a-reens', inhabitants of Gadara.

GADDI, gad'-di, fortunate.

GADDIEL, gad'-di-el, fortune of God (*i. e.*, sent from God).

GADITES, gad'-ites, descendants of Gad.

GAHAM, ga'-ham, sunburnt.

GAHAR, ga'-har, hiding-place.

GAIUS, ga'-yus, earthly.

GALAL, ga'-lal, weighty, worthy.

GALATIA, ga-la'-shya.

GALATIANS, ga-la'-shyans, inhabitants of Galatia.

GALEED, gal-e'ed, witness-heap.

GALILEE, gal'-i-lee, circuit.

GALLIM, gal'-lim, fountains.

GALLIO, gal'-li-o, one who lives on milk.

GAMALIEL, ga-ma'-li-el, benefit of God.

GAMMADIMS, gam'-ma-dims, warriors (?)

GAMUL, ga'-mul, weaned.

GAREB, ga'-reb, scabby.

GARMITE, gar'-mite, bony.

GASHMU, gash'-mu, (same as GESHEM, q. v.).

GATAM, ga'-tam, their touch, one puny or thin.

GATH, gath, wine-press.

GATH-RIMMON, gath-rim'-mon, *w.-p.* of the pomegranate.

GAZA, ga'-zah, strong, fortified.

GAZER, ga'-zer, place cut off, precipice.

GAZEZ, ga'-zez, shearer.

GAZITES, ga'-zites, inhabitants of Gaza.

GAZZAM, gaz'-zam, eating up.

GEBA, ge'-bah, hill.

GEBAL, ge'-bal, mountain.

GEBER, ge'-ber, man.

GEBIM, ge'-bim, (1) cisterns, or locusts, (2) trenches.

GEDALIAH, ged-a-li'-ah, whom Jehovah has made great.

GEDER, ge'-der, ｝ wall.
GEDOR, ge'-dor, ｝

GEDERAH, ged-e'-rah, enclosure, sheepfold.

GEDERITE, ged-e'-rite, native of Geder.

GEDEROTH, ged'-e-roth, folds.

GEHAZI, ge-ha'-zi, valley of vision

GELILOTH, gel-i'-loth, regions, borders.

GEMALLI, ge-mal'-li, possessor of driver of camels.

GEMARIAH, gem-a-ri'-ah, whom Jehovah has completed.

GENESIS, jen'-e-sis, generation, or beginning.

GENNESARET, gen-nes'-a-reth.

GENUBATH, gen-u'-bath, theft.

GENTILES, jen'-tiles, the nations of the west.

GERA, ｝ ge'-ra, a grain.
GERAH, ｝

GERAR, ge'-rar, sojourning, lodging-place.

GERGESENES, ger-ge-seens', inhabitants of Gerasa.

GERIZIM, ger-i'-zim.

GERSHOM, ger'-shom, ｝ expulsion.
GERSHON, ger'-shon, ｝

GESHAM, ge'-sham, filthy.

GESHEM, ge'-shem, is rained upon.

GESHUR, ge'-shur, bridge.

GESHURI, ge-shu'-ri, ｝ inhabitants of Geshur.
GESHURITES, ge-shu'-rites, ｝

GETHER, ge'-ther, dregs.

GETHSEMANE, geth-sem'-a-ne, oil-press.

GEUEL, gew'-el, majesty of God.

GEZER, ge'-zer, place cut off, precipice.

GEZRITES, gez'-rites, dwelling in a desert land.

GIAH, gi'-ah, breaking forth (*sc.*, of a fountain).

GINBAR, gib'-bar, a hero, a soldier.

GIBBETHON, gib'-be-thon, a lofty place, an acclivity.

GIBEA, ｝ gib'-e-ah, ｝ hill.
GIBEAH, ｝ ｝
GIBEATH, gib'-e-ath, ｝

GIBEON, gib'-e-on, pertaining to a hill (*i. e.*, built on a hill).

GIBEONITES, gib'-e-on-ites, inhabitants of Gibeon.

GIBLITES, gib'-lites, inhabitants of Gebal.

GIDDALTI, gid-dal'-ti, I have trained up.

GIDDEL, gid'-del, too great, giant.

GIDEON, gid'-e-on, cutter down (*i. e.*, brave soldier).

GIDEONI, gid-e-o'-ni, ｝ cutting down.
GIDOM, gi'-dom, ｝

GIHON, gi'-hon, breaking forth (of a river).

GILALAI, gi-la-lai', dungy.
GILBOA, gil-bo'-ah, bubbling fountain.
GILEAD, gil'-e-ad, (1) hard, stony region, (2) hill of witness.
GILEADITE, gil'-e-ad-ite, inhabitant of Gilead.
GILGAL, gil'-gal, a circle, or a rolling away.
GILOH, gi'-lo, emigration, exile.
GIMZO, gim'-zo, a place abounding with sycamores.
GINATH, gi'-nath, protection, garden.
GINNETHO, gin'-ne-tho, } gardener.
GINNETHON, gin'-ne-thon, } dener.
GIRGASHITE, gir'-gash-ite, dwelling in a clayey soil.
GISPA, gis'-pah, soothing, flattery.
GITTAH-HEPHER, git'-tah-he'-fer, wine-press of the well.
GITTAIM, git'-ta-im, two wine-presses.
GITTITES, git'-tites, inhabitants of Gath.
GITTITH, git'-tith, a stringed instrument.
GIZONITE, gi'-zo-nite.
GOATH, go'-ath, lowing.
GOB, gob, pit, cistern.
GOG, gog, extension.
GOLAN, go'-lan, exile.
GOLGOTHA, gol'-go-thah, a skull.
GOLIATH, go-li'-ath, exile, an exile.
GOMER, go'-mer, complete.
GOMORRAH, go-mor'-rah, culture, habitation.
GOSHEN, go'-shen, frontier (?)
GOZAN, go'-zan, stone quarry.
GREECE, grees', }
GRECIA, greesh'-ya, }
GUDGODAH, gud'-go-dah, thunder (?)
GUNI, gu'-ni, painted with colours.
GUNITES, gu'-nites, descendants of Guni.
GUR, gur, whelp, lion's cub.
GURBAAL, gur-ba'-al, sojourning of Baal.

HAAHASHTARI, ha-a-hash'-ta-ri, the muleteer.
HABAIAH, ha-bai'-ah, whom Jehovah hides.
HABAKKUK, hab'-bak-kuk, embrace.
HAB-AZINIAH, hab-az-i-ni'-ah, lamp of Jehovah.
HABOR, ha'-bor, joining together.
HACHALIAH, hak-a-li'-ah, whom Jehovah disturbs, dark.

HACHILAH, hak'-i-lah, dark, dusky.
HACHMONI, hak'-mo-ni, wise.
HACHMONITE, hak'-mo-nite, a descendant of Hachmoni.
HADAD, ha'-dad, sharpness.
HADADEZER, had-ad-e'-zer, whose help is Hadad.
HADAD-RIMMON, ha'-dad-rim'-mon, named from Hadad and Rimmon, q. v.
HADAR, ha'-dar, enclosure.
HADASHAH, had-a'-shah, new.
HADASSAH, had-as'-sah, myrtle.
HADATTAH, had-at'-tah, new.
HADID, ha'-did, sharp.
HADLAI, had'-lai, rest, rest of God.
HADORAM, ha-do'-ram, noble honour.
HADRACH, ha'-drak, dwelling.
HAGAB, ha'-gab, } locust.
HAGABA, ha-ga'-bah, } locust.
HAGAR, ha'-gar, flight.
HAGARITES, ha'-gar-ites.
HAGGAI, hag'-gai, } festive.
HAGGI, hag-gi, } festive.
HAGGERI, hag'-ger-i.
HAGGIAH, hag-gi'-ah, festival of Jehovah.
HAGGITES, hag'-gites, the posterity of Haggi.
HAGGITH, hag'-gith, festive, a dancer.
HAI, ha'-i, a heap of ruins.
HAKKATAN, hak-ka'-tan, the small.
HAKKOZ, hak'-koz, the thorn.
HAKUPHA, hak-u'-fah, bent.
HALA, ha'-lah.
HALAK, ha'-lak, smooth.
HALHUL, hal'-hul, trembling.
HALI, ha'-li, ornament, necklace.
HALLELUJAH, hal-le-loo'-yah, praise ye Jehovah.
HALLOHESH, hal-lo'-hesh, the enchanter.
HAM, ham, (1) warm, black, (2) noisy, multitude.
HAMAN, ha'-man, alone, solitary.
HAMATH, ha'-math, defence, citadel.
HAMATHITE, ha'-math-ite, a dweller at Hamath.
HAMATH-ZOBAH, ha'-math-zo'-bah.
HAMMATH, ham'-math, warm springs.
HAMMEDATHA, ham-med-a'-tha, twin (?)
HAMMELECH, ham-me'-lek, the king.
HAMMOLEKETH, ham-mo-le'-keth, the queen.
HAMMON, ham'-mon, warm, or sunny.

HAMMOTHDOR, ham'-moth-dor, warm-springs dwelling.

HAMONAH, ham-o'-nah, multitude.

HAMON-GOG, ha'-mon-gog, m. of Gog.

HAMOR, ha'-mor, ass.

HAMUEL, ham'-mu-el, heat (wrath) of God.

HAMUL, ha'-mul, who has experienced mercy.

HAMULITES, ha'-mul-ites, the posterity of Hamul.

HAMUTAL, ha-mu'-tal, refreshing like dew.

HANAMEEL, han'-a-me-el.

HANAN, ha'-nan, merciful.

HANANEEL, han'-a-ne-el, whom God graciously gave.

HANANI, ha-na'-ni, favourable, gracious.

HANANIAH, han-a-ni'-ah, whom Jehovah graciously gave.

HANES, ha'-nees.

HANIEL, han'-i-el, grace of God.

HANNAH, han'-nah, gracious.

HANNATHON, han'-na-thon, gracious.

HANNIEL, han'-ni-el, the favour of God.

HANOCH, ha'-nok, initiated.

HANOCHITES, ha'-nok-ites, descendants of Hanoch.

HANUN, ha'-nun, gracious, whom (God) pities.

HAPHRAIM, haf-ra'-im, two pits.

HARA, ha'-ra, mountainous.

HARADAH, har'-ra-dah, fear.

HARAN, ha'-ran, (1) mountaineer, (2) parched, dry.

HARARITE, har'-ra-rite, a mountaineer.

HARBONAH, har-bo'-nah, an ass-driver.

HAREPH, ha'-ref, plucking.

HARETH, ha'-reth, thicket.

HARHAIAH, har-hai'-yah, who was dried up.

HARHAS, har'-has, very poor.

HARHUR, har'-hur, inflammation.

HARIM, ha'-rim, flat-nosed.

HARIPH, ha'-rif, autumnal showers.

HARNEPHER, har-ne'-fer, to snore, to inhale, to pant.

HAROD, ha'-rod, fear, terror.

HARODITE, har'-ro-dite, inhabitant of Harod.

HAROEH, ha-ro'-eh, the seer.

HARORITE, har'-ro-rite. (See HARODITE.)

HAROSHETH, har-o'-sheth, carving or working.

HARSHA, har'-sha, enchanter, magician.

HARUM, ha'-rum, made high.

HARUMAPH, ha-ru'-maf, flat-nosed.

HARUPHITE, ha-ru'-fite.

HARUZ, ha'-ruz, eager, diligent.

HASADIAH, has-a-di'-ah, whom Jehovah loves.

HASENUAH, has-e-nu'-ah, the bristling.

HASHABIAH, hash-a-bi'-ah,
HASHABNAH, hash-ab'-nah,
HASHABNIAH, hash-ab-ni'-ah, } whom Jehovah esteems.

HASHBADANA, hash-bad-a'-na, thought in judging, wise judge.

HASHEM, ha'-shem, fat.

HASHMONAH, hash-mo'-nah, fatness, fat soil.

HASHUB, ha'-shub,
HASHUBAH, ha-shu'-bah, } understanding, considerate.

HASHUM, ha'-shum, rich, wealthy.

HASHUPHA, ha-shu'-fa, made naked.

HASRAH, haz'-rah, very poor.

HASSENAAH, has-se-na'-ah, the thorny.

HATACH, ha'-tak, verity.

HATHATH, ha'-thath, terror.

HATIPHA, hat'-i-fah, seized, captive.

HATITA, hat'-i-tah, digging, exploring.

HATTIL, hat'-til, wavering.

HATTUSH, hat'-tush, assembled.

HAVILAH, hav-i'-lah, puny terror.

HAVOTH-JAIR, ha'-voth-ja'-ir, villages of Jair.

HAURAN, haw'-ran, cave-land.

HAZAEL, haz'-a-el, whom God watches over.

HAZAIAH, haz-ai'-ah, whom Jehovah watches over.

HAZAR-ADDAR, ha'-zar-ad'-dar, village of Addar.

HAZAR-ENAN, ha'-zar-e'-nan, v. of fountains.

HAZAR-GADDAH, ha'-zar-gad' dah, v. of good fortune.

HAZAR-HATTICON, ha'-zar-hat'-ti-kon, middle v.

HAZAR-MAVETH, ha'-zar-ma'-veth, court of death.

HAZAR-SHUAL, ha'-zar-shu'-al, village of jackals.

HAZAR-SUSIM, ha'-zar-su'-sim, v. of (station for) horses.

HAZELEL-PONI, ha'-zel-el-po'-ni, the shadow looking on me.

HAZERIM, ha-ze'-rim, } villages.
HAZEROTH, haz-e'-roth,

HAZER-SHUSIM, ha'-zer-shu'-sim, the village of horses.

HAZEZON-TAMAR, ha'-ze-zon-ta'mar, pruning of the palm.

HAZIEL, ha'-zi-el, the vision of God, seen by God.

HAZO, ha'-zo, vision.

HAZOR, ha'-zor, enclosure, castle.

HEBER, he'-ber, (1) a passer over, (2) fellowship, society.

HEBREWS, he'-brews, descendants of Eber.

HEBRON, he'-bron, conjunction, joining, alliance.

HEBRONITES, he'-bron-ites, the people of Hebron.

HEGAI, he-ga'-i, venerable (?)

HELAH, he'-lah, rust.

HELAM, he'-lam, stronghold.

HELBAH, hel'-bah, fatness (i. e., a fertile region).

HELBON, hel'-bon, fat (i. e., fertile).

HELDAI, hel'-dai, worldly, terrestrial, vital.

HELEB, he'-leb, (same as HELBAH, q. v.).

HELED, he'-led, life, the world.

HELEK, he'-lek, portion.

HELEKITES, he'-lek-ites, descendants of Helek.

HELEM, he'-lem, stroke.

HELEPH, he'-lef, exchange.

HELEZ, he'-lez, loin, liberation.

HELI, he'-li, summit.

HELKAI, hel'-kai, Jehovah his portion.

HELKATH, hel'-kath, a portion.

HELKATH-HAZZURIM, hel'-kath-haz'-zu-rim, the p. (field) of swords.

HELON, he'-lon, strong.

HEMAN, he'-man, faithful.

HEMATH, he'-math, fortress.

HEMDAN, hem'-dan, pleasant.

HEN, hen, favour.

HENA, he'-nah, low ground.

HENADAD, hen'-a-dad, favour of Hadad.

HENOCH, he'-nok. (See ENOCH.)

HEPHER, he'-fer, pit, well.

HEPHERITES, he'-fer-ites, descendants of Hepher.

HEPHZIBAH, hef'-zi-bah, in whom is my delight.

HERES, he'-res, the sun.

HERESH, he'-resh, artificer.

HERMAS, her'-mas, Mercury.

HERMOGENES, her-moj'-e-neez, descendant of Mercury.

HERMON, her'-mon, lofty.

HERMONITES, her'-mon-ites, (the summits of Hermon are meant).

HEROD, her'-rod, glory of the skin.

HERODIANS, he-ro'-di-ans, partisans of Herod.

HERODIAS, he-ro'-di-as, mount of pride.

HERODION, he-ro'-di-on.

HESHBON, hesh'-bon, device.

HESHMON, hesh'-mon, fatness, fat soil.

HETH, heth, fear, terror.

HETHLON, heth'-lon, a hiding-place, a place wrapped up.

HEZEKI, hez'-e-ki, strong.

HEZEKIAH, hez-e-ki'-ah, the might of Jehovah (i. e., given by Jehovah).

HEZIR, he'-zir, swine.

HEZION, hez'-i-on, vision.

HEZRAI, hez'-rai, } enclosed, surrounded by a wall.
HEZRON, hez'-ron,

HEZRONITES, hez'-ron-ites, descendants of Hezron.

HIDDAI, hid'-dai, for the rejoicing of Jehovah.

HIDDEKEL, hid'-de-kel, active, vehement, rapid.

HIEL, hi'-el, God liveth.

HIERAPOLIS, hi-er-rap'-o-lis, a sacred or holy city.

HILEN, hi'-len, place of caves.

HILKIAH, hil-ki'-ah, portion of Jehovah.

HILLEL, hil'-lel, singing, praising.

HINNOM, hin'-nom.

HIRAH, hi'-rah, nobility. a noble race.

HIRAM, hi'-ram, noble.

HIZKIAH, hiz-ki'-ah, } might of
HIZKIJAH, hiz-ki'-jah, } Jehovah.

HITTITES, hit'-tites, descendants of Heth.

HIVITES, hi'-vites, belonging to a village.

HOBAB, ho'-bab, beloved.

HOBAH, ho'-bah, a hiding-place.

HOD, hod, splendour.

HODAIAH, ho-dai'-yah, } praise
HODAVIAH, ho-da-vi'-ah, } ye Jehovah, or Jehovah His glory.

HODESH, ho'-desh, new moon.

HODEVAH, ho'-de-va, (same as HO-
DAVIAH, q.v.).
HODIAH, ho-di'-ah, } majesty of
HODIJAH, ho-di'-jah, } God.
HOGLAH, hog'-lah, partridge.
HOHAM, ho'-ham, whom Jehovah
impels.
HOLON, ho-lon, sandy.
HOMAM, ho'-mam, destruction.
HOPHNI, hof'-ni, pugilist, fighter.
HOPHRAH, hof'-rah (see PHARAOH-
H.)
HOR, hor, mountain.
HORAM, ho'-ram, height, mountain-
ous.
HOREB, ho'-reb, dry, desert.
HOREM, ho'-rem, devoted, sacred.
HORHAGIDGAD, hor'-ha-gid'-gad,
conspicuous mountain.
HORI, ho'-ri, cave-dweller.
HORIMS, ho'-rims, } descendants of
HORITES, ho'-rites, } Hori.
HORMAH, hor'-mah, a devoting, a
place laid waste.
HORONAIM, hor-o-na'-im, two ca-
verns.
HORONITE, hor'-o-nite, native of
Horonaim.
HOSAH, ho'-sah, fleeing for refuge,
or a refuge.
HOSEA, ho-ze'-ah, } welfare, salva-
HOSHEA, ho-she'-a, } tion.
HOSHAIAH, ho-shai'-yah, whom
Jehovah aids, whom Jehovah has set
free.
HOSHAMA, hosh'-a-mah, whom
Jehovah hears.
HOTHAM, ho'-tham, } signet ring.
HOTHAN, ho'-than, }
HOTHIR, ho'-thur, (whom Jehovah)
left (?)
HUKKOK, huk'-kok, decreed.
HUL, hull, circle.
HULDAH, hul'-dah, a mole, weasel.
HUMTAH, hum'-tah, place of lizards.
HUPHAM, hu'-fam, inhabitant of the
shore.
HUPHAMITES, hu'-fam-ites, descen-
dants of Hupham.
HUPPAH, hup-pah, covering.
HUPPIM, hup'-pim, coverings.
HUR, hur, cavern.
HURAI, hu'-rai, linen-worker.
HURAM, hu'-ram, noble, free-born (?)
HURI, hu'-ri, linen-worker.
HUSHAH, hu'-shah, haste.
HUSHAI, hu'-sha, hasting.

HUSHAM, hu'-sham, haste.
HUSHATHITE, hu'-shath-ite, inhabi-
tant of Hushah.
HUSHIM, hu'-shim, those who make
haste.
HUZ, huz, eight, sandy soil.
HUZZAB, huz'-zab.
HYMENEUS, hy-men-e'-us, nuptial,
or a wedding song.

IBHAR, ib'-har, whom He (sc. God)
chooses.
IBLEAM, ib'-le-am, devouring the
people.
IBNEIAH, ib-nei'-yah, } whom Jeho-
IBNIJAH, ib-ni'-jah, } vah will build
up, i.e., cause to prosper.
IBRI, ib'-ri, Hebrew.
IBZAN, ib'-zan, tin.
ICHABOD, ik'-a-bod, inglorious.
ICONIUM, i-ko'-ni-um.
IDALAH, id'-a-lah, that which God
has shown.
IDBASH, id'-bash, honied.
IDDO, id'-do (1) loving, given to love;
(2) calamity.
IDUMÆA, i-du-me'-ah (same as EDOM
q.v.)
IGAL, i'-gal, whom God will avenge.
IGEAL, i'-ge-al.
IGDALIAH, ig-da-li'-ah, whom Jeho-
vah shall make great.
IIM, i'-im, ruins.
IJE-ABARIM, i-je-ab'-a-rim, ruinous
heaps of Abarim.
IJON, i'-jon, a ruin.
IMLAH, im'-lah, whom He (God) will
fill up.
IKKESH, ik'-kesh, perverseness of
mouth.
ILLYRICUM, il-lirr'-i-kum.
IMMANUEL, im-man'-u-el, God with
us.
IMMER, im'-mer, talking, loquacious.
IMNA, } im'-nash, whom He (God)
IMNAH, } keeps back.
IMRAH, im'-rah, stubborn.
IMRI, im'-ri, eloquent.
INDIA, in'-dya, land of the Indus.
IPHEDEIAH, if-e-di'-ah, whom Jeho-
vah frees.
IR, eer, city.
IRA, i'-rah, town, watchful.
IRAD, i'-rad, wild ass.
IRAM, i'-ram, } belonging to a city
IRI, i'-ri, }

IRIJAH, i-ri'-jah, whom Jehovah looks on.
IRON, i'-ron, timid, pious, piety.
IRPEEL, eer'-pe-el, which God heals.
IRSHEMISH, eer-she'-mesh, city of the sun.
IRU, i'-ru.
ISAAC, i'-zak, laughter, sporting.
ISAIAH, i-zai'-yah, the salvation of Jehovah.
ISCAH, is'-kah, one who beholds, looks out.
ISCARIOT, is-kar'-ri-ot, man of Keristh.
ISHBAH, ish'-bah, praising.
ISHBAK, ish'-bak, leaving behind.
ISHBI-BENOB, ish'-bi-be'-nob, his seat is at Nob, my seat is at Nob.
ISHBOSHETH, ish-bo'-sheth, man of shame, i.e., shaming himself, perhaps bashful.
ISHI, ish'-i, salutary.
ISHIAH, ish-i'-ah, } whom Jehovah
ISHIJAH, ish-i'-jah, } lends.
ISHMA, ish'-ma, wasteness.
ISHMAEL, ish'-ma-el, whom God hears.
ISHMAELITES, ish'-ma-el-ites, } de-
ISHMEELITES, ish'-me-el-ites, } scendants of Jehovah.
ISMAIAH, iz-mai'-yah, } whom J.
ISHMAIAH, ish-mai'-yah, } hears.
ISHMERAI, ish'-me-rai, whom J. keeps.
ISHOD, ish'-od, man of glory.
ISHPAN, ish'-pan, bald.
ISHTOB, ish'-tob, men of Job.
ISHUAH, ish-u'-ah, } even, level.
ISHUI, ish'-u-i, }
ISMACHIAH, is-ma-ki'-ah, whom Jehovah props up.
ISRAEL, iz'-ra-el, contender or soldier of God.
ISRAELITES, iz'-ra-el-ites, descendants of Israel.
ISSACHAR, is'-sa-kar, he brings wages (?)
ITALY, it'-a-ly.
ITHAI, i'-thai, with the Lord.
ITHAMAR, ith'-a-mar, land of palms.
ITHIEL, ith'-i-el, God is with me.
ITHMAH, ith'-mah, bereavedness.
ITHNAN, ith'-nan, given.
ITHRA, ith'-rah, } excellence.
ITHRAN, ith'-ran, }
ITHREAM, ith'-re-am, abundance of people, rest of the people.

ITHRITE, ith'-rite, descendants of Jether (?)
ITTAH-KAZIN, it'-tah-ka'-zin, time of the judge, people of the judge.
ITTAI, it'-tai, with the Lord.
ITUREA, it-u-re'-ah, a province named from Jetur.
IVAH, i'-vah, overturning.
IZHAR, } iz'-e-har, } oil.
IZEHAR, } iz'-har, }
IZRAHIAH, iz-ra-hi'-ah, whom Jehovah brought to light.
IZRAHITE, iz'-ra-hite, probably same as ZARHITE, q. v.
IZRI, iz'-ri, the Izrite or Jezerite.

JAAKAN, ja'-a-kan, he shall surround.
JAAKOBAH, ja-ak-o'-bah, taking hold of the heel, supplanter, layer of snares.
JAALA, ja'-a-la, wild she-goat.
JAALAM, ja'-a-lam, whom God hides.
JAANAI, ja'-an-ai, whom Jehovah answers.
JAAREOREGIM, ja'-ar-e-or'-e-gim, forests of the weavers.
JAASAU, ja'-a-saw, whom Jehovah made.
JAASIEL, ja-a'-si-el, whom God comforts.
JAAZANIAH, ja-az-za-ni'-ah, whom Jehovah hears.
JAAZER, ja'-a-zer, whom He (God) aids.
JAAZIAH, ja-a-zi'-ah, which Jehovah comforts.
JABAL, ja'-bal, stream.
JABBOK, jab'-bok, pouring out, emptying.
JABESH, ja'-besh, dry.
JABESH-GILEAD, ja'-besh-gil'-e-ad, Jabesh of Gilead.
JABEZ, ja'-bez, causing pain.
JABIN, ja'-bin, whom He (God) considered.
JABNEEL, jab'-ne-el, which God caused to be built.
JABNEH, jab'-neh, which He (God) caused to be built.
JACHAN, ja'-kan, troubled.
JACHIN, ja'kin, whom God strengthens, founds.
JACOB, ja'-kob, taking hold of the heel, supplanter.
JADA, ja'-dah, wise.
JADAU, ja'-daw, loving.
JADDUA, jad'-du-a, known.
JADON, ja'-don, a judge, or whom God has judged.
JAEL, ja'-el, mountain goat.

JAGUR, ja'-gur, lodging.
JAH, jah (poetic form of Jehovah, q. v.)
JAHATH, ja'-hath, union.
JAHAZ, ja'-haz, ⎫
JAHAZA, ⎬ ja'-haz-ah, ⎫ a place trampled
JAHAZAH, ⎭ ⎬ down, per-
haps a threshing floor.
JAHAZIAH, ja-ha-zi'-ah, whom Jehovah watches over.
JAHAZIEL, ja-haz'-i-el, whom God watches over.
JAHDAI, jah'-dai, whom Jehovah directs.
JAHDIEL, jah'-di-el, whom God makes glad.
JAHDO, jah'-do, united, his union.
JAHLEEL, jah'-le-el, hoping in God.
JAHLEELITES, jah-le-el-ites, descendants of Jahleel.
JAHMAI, jah'-mai, whom Jehovah guards.
JAHZAH, jah'-zah.
JAHZEEL, jah'-ze-el, whom God allots.
JAHZEELITES, jah'-ze-el-ites, descendants of Jahzeel.
JAHZERAH, jah'-ze-rah, whom God brings back.
JAIR, ja'-er, whom He (sc. God) enlightens.
JAIRUS, ja'-i-rus (Greek form of Jair).
JAKAN, ja'-kan, see JAAKAN.
JAKEH, ja'-keh, pious.
JAKIM, ja'-kim, whom God sets up.
JALON, ja'-lon, passing the night, tarrying.
JAMBRES, jam'-brees.
JAMES, james, supplanter, underminer.
JAMIN, ja'-min, right hand.
JAMINITES, ja'-min-ites, descendants of Jamin.
JAMLECH, jam'-lek, whom God makes to reign.
JANNA, jan'-na, whom Jehovah bestows.
JANNES, jan'-nees.
JANOAH, ja-no'-ah, ⎫
JANOHAH, ja-no'-hah, ⎬ rest.
JANUM, ja'-num, sleep, flight.
JAPHETH, ja'-feth, widely extending.
JAPHIA, ja-fi'-ah, splendid.
JAPHLET, jaf'-let, whom God frees.
JAPHLETI, jaf-le'-ti, the Jafletite.
JAPHO, ja'-fo, beauty.
JARAH, ja'-rah, honey.

JAREB, ja'-reb, adversary.
JARED, ja'-red, descent.
JARESIAH, ja-re-si'-ah, whom Jehovah nourishes.
JARHA, jar'-ha.
JARIB, ja'-rib, adversary.
JARMUTH, jar'-muth, high.
JAROAH, ja-ro'-ah, moon.
JASHEN, ja'-shen, sleeping.
JASHER, ja'-sher, upright.
JASHOBEAM, ja-sho'-be-am, to whom the people turn.
JASHUB, ja'-shub, turning oneself.
JASHUBI-LEHEM, ja-shu'-bi-le'-hem, a returner to Bethlehem.
JASHUBITES, ja'-shu-bites, descendants of Jashut.
JASIEL, ja-si'-el, whom God made.
JASON, ja'-son, healing, or one who gives medicines.
JATHNIEL, jath'-ni-el, whom God gives.
JATTIR, jat'-teer, height.
JAVAN, ja'-van, clay.
JAZER, ja'-zer, whom (God) aids.
JAZIZ, ja'-ziz, whom (God) moves; to whom God gives life and motion).
JEARIM, je-a'-rim, forests.
JEATERAI, jea'-te-rai, whom the Lord shall cause to stay.
JBDERECHIAH, jeb-er-re-ki'-ah, whom Jehovah blesses.
JEBUS, je'-bus, a place trodden down, as a threshing floor.
JEBUSI, jeb'-u-si (from Jebus).
JEBUSITES, jeb'-u-sites, the descendants of Jebus, the son of Canaan.
JECAMIAH, jek-a-mi'-ah, whom Jehovah gathers.
JECOLIAH, jek-o-li'-ah, for whom J. shows Himself strong, strong by means of J.
JECONIAH, jek-o-ni'-ah, whom J. has appointed.
JEDAIAH, je-dai'-yah, who praises J.
JEDIAEL, jed-i'-a-el, known by God.
JEDIDAH, jed-i'-dah, beloved.
JEDIDIAH, jed-i-di'-ah, the delight (friend) of Jehovah.
JEDUTHUN, jed-u'-thun, praising, celebrating.
JEEZER, je-e'-zer (extracted from ABIEZER, q. v.).
JEEZORITES, je-o'-zor-ites, descendants of Jeezer.
JEGAR-SAHADUTHA, je'-gar-sa-ha-du'-thah, the heap of witness (?)

JEHALELEEL, je-hal'-el-e-el,) who
JEHALELEL, je-hal'-e-lel,   } praises
                              } God.
JEHDEIAH, jeh-dei'-yah, whom Jeho-
vah makes glad.
JEHIEL, je-hi'-el, whom God pre-
serves alive, God liveth.
JEHIELI, je-hi-e'-li, a Jehielite.
JEHEZEKEL, je-hez'-e-kel (same as
EZEKIEL, q. v.).
JEHIAH, je-hi'-ah, Jehovah lives.
JEHISKIAH, je-hiz-ki'-ah, Jehovah
strengthens.
JEHOADAH, je-ho'-a-dah,) whom J.
JEHOADDAN, je-ho'-a-dan, } adorned.
JEHOAHAZ, je-ho'-a-haz, whom J.
holds fast.
JEHOASH, je-ho'-ash,   ) whom
JEHOHANAN, je-ho-ha'-nan, } J.gave.
JEHOIACHIN, je-hoy'-a-kin, whom J.
has established.
JEHOIADA, je-hoy'-a-dah, whom J.
cared for.
JEHOIAKIM, je-hoy'-a-kim, whom J.
has set up.
JEHOIARIB, je-hoy'-a-rib, whom J.
will defend.
JEHONADAB, je-hon'-a-dab, whom J.
impels.
JEHONATHAN, je-hon'-a-than (see
JONATHAN).
JEHORAM, je-ho'-ram, whom J. up-
holds.
JEHOSHABEATH, je-ho-shab'-e-ath
whose oath is J.
JEHOSHAPHAT, je-hosh'-a-fat, whom
J. judges (pleads for).
JEHOSHEBA, je-hosh'-e-ba, whose
oath is J.
JEHOSHUA, je-hosh'-u-a (see
JOSHUA).
JEHOVAH, je-ho'-vah, the eternal,
the immutable is His name.
JEHOVAH-JIREH, je-ho'-vah-ji'-reh,
J. will see or provide.
JEHOVAH-NISSI, je-ho'-vah-nis'-si, J.
my banner.
JEHOVAH-SHALLOM,   je-ho'-vah-
shal'-lom, J. send peace.
JEHOVAH-SHAMMAH,   je-ho'-vah-
sham'-mah, J. is there.
JEHOVAH-TSIDKENU,   jeho'-vah-
tsid-ke'-nu, J. our righteousness.
JEHOZABAD, je-hoz'-a-bad, whom J.
gave.
JEHOZADAK, je-hoz'-a-dak, whom J.
makes just.
JEHU, je'-hu, Jehovah is He.
JEHUBBAH, je-hub'-bah, hidden (i.e.,
protected).

JEHUCAL, je-hu'-cal, able.
JEHUD, je'-hud, praised.
JEHUDI, je-hu'-di, a Jew.
JEHUDIJAH, je-hu-di-'jah,   the
Jewess.
JEHUSH, je'-hush, to whom God
hastens.
JEIEL, jei'-el, treasured of God (?)
JEKABZEEL, je-kab'-ze-el, what God
gathers.
JEKAMEAM, jek-am'-e-am, who ga-
thers the people together.
JEKAMIAH, jek-a-mi'-ah, whom Je-
hovah gathers.
JEKUTHIEL, je-ku'-thi-el, the fear
of God.
JEMIMA, je-mi'-ma, dove.
JEMUEL, jem-u'-el, day of God.
JEPHTHAH, jef'-thah, whom, or
what God sets free.
JEPHUNNEH, je-fun'-neh, for whom
a way is prepared.
JERAH, je'-rah, the moon.
JERAHMEEL, jer-ah'-me-el, whom
God loves.
JERAHMEELITES, jer-ah'-me-el-ites,
descendants of Jerahmeel.
JERED, je'-red, descent.
JEREMAI, jer'-e-mi, dwelling in
heights.
JEREMIAH, jer-e-mi'-ah, whom Je-
hovah has appointed.
JEREMOTH, je-re'-moth, high places
JERIAH, je-ri'-ah, people of Jehovah,
either founded by God, or else, whom
Jehovah regards.
JERICHO, jer'-i-ko, a fragrant place.
JERIEL, je-ri'-el, people of God,
founded by God.
JERIJAH, je-ri'-jah, people of Jeho-
vah, either founded by God, or else,
whom Jehovah regards.
JERIMOTH, jer'-i-moth, heights.
JERIOTH, je-ri'-oth, curtains.
JEROHAM, jer-o'-ham, who is loved,
who will find mercy.
JEROBOAM, jer-o-bo'-am, whose peo-
ple are many.
JERUBBAAL, je-rub'-ba-al, let Baal
plead.
JERUEL, je-ru'-el, people, or habita-
tion of God, founded by God.
JERUSALEM, je-ru'-sa-lem, the pos-
session, habitation, or vision of peace.
JERUSHA, je-ru'-sha, possessed, sc.,
by a husband.
JESHAIAH, je-shai'-yah,) the salva-
JESAIAH, je-sai'-yah.   } tion of Je-
                          } hovah

JESHANAH, jesh-a'-nah, old.
JESHARELAH, jesh-ar-e'-lah, right before God.
JESHEBEAB, jesh-e'-be-ab, father's seat.
JESHER, je'-sher, uprightness.
JESHIMON, jesh-i'-mon, the waste.
JESHISHAI, jesh-i'-shai, descended from an old man.
JESHOHAIAH, jesh-o-hai'-yah, whom Jehovah casts down.
JESHUA, jesh'-u-ah, J. the salvation.
JESHURUN, jesh-u'-run, supremely happy.
JESIAH, je-si'-ah.
JESIMIEL, jes-im'-mi-el, whom God makes, i. e., creates.
JESSE, jes'-se, wealthy.
JESUI, jes'-u-i, even, level.
JESUITES, jes'-u-ites, the posterity of Jesui.
JESUS, je'-sus, Saviour.
JETHER, je'-ther.
JETHETH, je'-theth, a nail.
JETHLAH, jeth'-lah, height, lofty place.
JETHRO, jeth'-ro, his excellence.
JETUR, je'-tur, an enclosure, an encampment of Nomades.
JEUSH, je'-ush (to whom God) hastens.
JEUZ, je'-uz, counsellor.
JEWRY, ju'-ry, the country of Judea.
JEWS, jews, inhabitants of Judea.
JEZANIAH, jez-a-ni'-ah.
JEZEBEL, jez'-e-bel, without cohabitation.
JEZER, je'-zer, power, imagination.
JEZIAH, je-zi'-ah, whom Jehovah sprinkles, expiates.
JEZIEL, je-zi'-el, the assembly of God.
JEZLIAH, jez-li'-ah, whom God draws out (i. e., will preserve).
JEZOAR, je-zo'-ar, whiteness.
JEZRAHIAH, jez-ra-hi'-ah, whom Jehovah brings forth.
JEZREEL, jez'-re-el, that which God planted.
JIBSAM, jib'-sam, pleasant.
JIDLAPH, jid'-laf, weeping.
JIMNAH, jim'-nah, prosperity.
JIMNITES, jim'-nites, descendants of Jimna or Jimnah.
JIPHTAH, jif'-tah, whom, or what God sets free.
JIPHTHAHEL, jif'-tha-hel, which God opens.

JOAB, jo'-ab, whose father is Jehovah.
JOAH, jo'-ah, whose brother (i. e., helper) is J.
JOAHAZ, jo-a'-haz, whom J. holds.
JOANNA, jo-an'-nah, grace or gift of J.
JOASH, jo'-ash, whom J. bestowed and whom J. hastens.
JOB, jobe, (1) a desert, (2) one persecuted.
JOBAB, jo'-bab, a desert.
JOCHEBED, jok'-e-bed, whose glory is Jehovah.
JOED, jo'-ed, for whom J. is witness.
JOEL, jo'-el, to whom J. is God.
JOELAH, jo-e'-lah, he helps, or J aids him.
JOEZER, jo-e'-zer, whose help is J.
JOGBEAH, jog'-be-ah, lofty.
JOGLI, jog'-li, led into exile.
JOHA, jo'-ha, whom Jehovah called back to life (?)
JOHANAN, jo-ha'-nan, whom J. bestowed.
JOHN, jon, the grace or gift of God, whom J. bestows.
JOIADA, joy'-a-dah, whom J. favours.
JOIAKIM, joy'-a-kim } whom J. sets
JOKIM, jo'-kim,   }   up.
JOIARIB, joy'-a-rib, whom J. defends.
JOKDEAM, jok'-de-am, possessed by the people.
JOKMEAM, jok-me'-am, or jok'-me-am, gathered by the p.
JOKNEAM, jok'-ne-am, or jok-ne'-am, possessed by the p.
JOKSHAN, jok'-shan, fowler.
JOKTAN, jok'-tan, small.
JOKTHEEL, jok-the'-el, subdued by God.
JONADAB, jon'-a-dab, whom Jehovah impels.
JONAH, jo'-nah, dove.
JONAN, jo'-nan (contracted from JOHANAN, q. v.)
JONATHAN, jon'-a-than, whom Jehovah gave.
JOPPA, jop'-pah, beauty (?)
JORAH, jo'-rah, watering: the former rain.
JORAI, jo'-rai, whom Jehovah teaches.
JORAM, jo'-ram, whom J. is exalted.
JORDAN, jor'-dan, descending, flowing down.
JORIM, jo'-rim (a form of Joram ?)

JORKOAM, jor'-ko-am, paleness of the people (?)

JOSABAD, jos'-a-bad, whom Jehovah bestows.

JOSEDECH, jos'-e-dek, towards whom J. is just, whom J. has made just.

JOSES, jo'-sees, (1) sparing, exalted, (2) whom J. helps.

JOSEPH, jo'-seph, he shall add.

JOSHAH, jo'-shah, } whom J. allows to
JOSHAVIAH, josh-a-vi'-ah } dwell.

JOSHAPHAT, josh'-a-fat. (See JE-HOSHAPHAT.)

JOSHBEKASHAH, josh-bek-a'-shah, a seat in a hard place.

JOSHUA, josh'-u-a, whose help is Jehovah.

JOSIAH, jo-si'-ah, whom J. heals.

JOSIBIAH, jos-i-bi'-ah, to whom God gives a dwelling.

JOSIPHIAH, jos-i-fi'-ah, whom Jehovah will increase.

JOTBAH, jot'-bah, }
JOTBATH, jot'-bath, } good-
JOTBATHAH, jot'-ba-thah, } ness.

JOTHAM, jo'-tham, Jehovah is upright.

JOZACHAR, joz'-a-kar, whom J. has remembered.

JOZADAK, joz'-a-dak, whom J. has made just.

JUBAL, ju'-bal, music.

JUCAL, ju'-cal, potent.

JUDAH, ju'-dah, }
JUDAS, ju'-das, } praised.
JUDE, jood, }

JUDEA, ju-de'-a, from Judah.

JUDITH, ju'-dith (probably from the same).

JULIA, ju'-li-a (feminine of JULIUS).

JULIUS, ju'-li-us.

JUNIA, ju'-ni-a, youthful, or belonging to Juno.

JUPITER, ju'-pi-ter, helping father.

JUSHAB-HESED, ju'-shab-he'-sed, whose love is returned.

JUSTUS, jus'-tus, upright, righteous.

JUTTAH, jut'-tah, stretched out, or inclined.

KABZEEL, kab'-ze-el, which God gathers.

KADESH, ka'-desh, sacred.

KADESH-BARNEA, ka'-desh-bar'-ne-a sacred desert of wandering.

KADMIEL, kad'-mi-el, one before (a minister of) God.

KADMONITES, kad'-mon-ites, Orientals.

KALLAI, kal'-lai, the swift (servant) of Jehovah.

KANAH, ka'-nah, a place of reed.

KAREAH, ka-re'-ah, bald.

KARKAA, kar-ka'-ah, } foundation,
KARKER, kar'-ker, } bottom, soft, and level ground.

KARNAIM, kar-na'-im, two horns.

KARTAH, kar'-tah, city.

KARTAN, kar'-tan, two towns, double town or city.

KEDAR, ke'-dar, black-skinned.

KEDEMAH, ke'-de-mah, eastward.

KEDEMOTH, ke'-de-moth, beginnings.

KEDESH, ke'-desh, sanctuary.

KEHELATHAH, ke-he'-la-thath, assembly.

KEILAH, ki'-lah, fortress.

KELAIAH, ke-lai'-yah, swift messenger of Jehovah.

KELITA, kel-i'-tah, (1) assembly; (2) dwarf.

KEMUEL, kem'-u-el, congregation of God.

KENAN, ke'-nan, (1) possession, (2) smith.

KENATH, ke'-nath, possession.

KENAZ, ke'-naz, hunting.

KENEZITE, ken'-e-zite, descendants of Kenaz (?)

KENITES, ke'-nites, } smiths,
KENNIZZITES, ken'-iz-ites, } dwellers in a nest.

KERENHAPPUCH, ke'-ren-hap-puk, horn of paint.

KERIOTH, ker'-i-oth, cities.

KEROS, ke'-ros, a weaver's comb.

KETURAH, ke-tu'-rah, incense.

KEZIA, ke-zi'-a, cassia.

KEZIZ, ke'-ziz, cut off.

KIBROTH-HATTAAVAH, kib'-roth-hat-ta'-a-vah, graves of lust.

KIBZAIM, kib'-za-im, two heaps.

KIDRON, kid'-ron, or ki'-dron, turbid.

KINAH, ki'-nah, song of mourning, lamentation.

KIR, keer, wall, walled place.

KIRHARASETH, kir-har-a'-seth, }
KIRHARESH, kir-ha'-resh, }
KIRHERES, kir-he'-res, }
brick fortress.

KIRIOTH, kir'-e-oth, cities.

KIRJATH, keer'-jath, city (?)

KIRJATHARBA, keer'-jath-ar'-bah, city of Arba.

KIRJATH-AIM, keer'-jath-a'-im, double city.

KIRJATH-ARIM, keer'-jath-a'-rim (contracted from K.-JEARIM, q. v.)

KIRJATH-BAAL, keer'-jath-ba'-al, city of Baal.

KIRJATH-HUZOTH, keer'-jath-hu'-zoth, c. of streets.

KIRJATH-JEARIM, keer'-jath-je'-a-rim, c. of woods.

KIRJATH-SANNAH, keer'-jath-san'-nah, c. of palm trees.

KIRJATH-SEPHER, keer'-jath-se'-fer, book-c.

KISH, kish, snaring, a bow.

KISHI, kish'-i, bow of Jehovah.

KISHION, kish'-i-on, } hardness.
KISHON, kish'-on,

KISHON, ki'-shon, twisted, tortuous.

KITHLISH, kith'-lish, man's wall.

KITRON, kit'-ron, bond, knotty.

KITTIM, kit'-tim (see CHITTIM).

KOA, ko'-a, stallion, he camel.

KOHATH, ko'-hath, assembly.

KOHATHITES, ko'-hath-ites, descendants of Kohath.

KOLAIAH, kol-ai'-yah, voice of Jehovah.

KORAH, ko'-rah, ice, hail, baldness.

KORE, ko'-re, partridge.

KOZ, koz, thorn.

KUSHAIAH, kush-ai'-yah, bow of Jehovah (i. e., the rainbow.)

LAADAH, la'-a-dah, order.

LAADAN, la'-a-dan, put into order.

LABAN, la'-ban, white.

LACHISH, la'-kish, obstinate (i. e., hard to be captured).

LAEL, la'-el, by God (created).

LAHAD, la'-had, oppression.

LAHAIROI, la-hah'-y-ro'-y, the living One that sees me.

LAHMAM, lah'-mam, provisions.

LAHMI, lah'-mi, warrior.

LAISH, la'-ish, lion.

LAKUM, la'-kum, stopping up the way.

LAMECH, la'-mek, powerful.

LAODICEA, la-od-i-se'-ah,

LAODICEANS, la-od-i-se'-ans, inhabitants of Laodicea.

LAPIDOTH, lap'-i-doth, torches.

LASEA, la-se'-ah,

LASHAH, la'-shah, fissure.

LASHARON, la-sha'-ron, the plain.

LAZARUS, laz'-a-rus, helpless, helped of God.

LEAH, le'-ah, wearied.

LEBANAH, le-ba'-nah, } the white.
LEBANON, leb'-a-non,

LEBAOTH, leb'-a-oth, lionesses.

LEBBEUS, leb-be'-us, a man of heart, praising or confessing.

LEBONAH, le-bo'-nah, frankincense

LECAH, le'-kah, progress, journey.

LEHABIM, le-ha'-bim, (see LUBIM)

LEHI, le'-hi, jaw-bone.

LEMUEL, lem'-u-el, by God created.

LESHEM, le'-shem, precious stone.

LETUSHIM, le-tu'-shim, the hammered.

LEUMMIN, le-um'-min, peoples.

LEVI, le'-vi, adhesion, or garland, crown.

LEVITES, le'-vites, descendants of Levi.

LEVITICUS, le-vit'-i-cus (from the foregoing word).

LIBERTINES, li-ber'-tines, made free.

LIBNAH, lib'-nah, whiteness.

LIBNI, lib'-ni, white.

LIBYA, lib'-ya,

LIKHI, lik'-hi, learned, imbued with learning.

LINUS, li'-nus, a net.

LOAMMI, lo-am'-mi, not my people.

LOD, lod, contention, strife.

LODEBAR, lo'-de-bar, without pasture.

LOIS, lo'-is, better.

LO-RUHAMAH, lo-ru'-ha-mah, not having obtained mercy.

LOT, lot, covering, veil.

LOTAN, lo'-tan, a wrapping-up.

LUBIM, lu'-bim, dwellers in a scorched land (?)

LUCAS, lu'-kas (see LUKE).

LUCIFER, lu'-si-fer, light-bearer.

LUCIUS, lu'-shi-us, of light.

LUD, lud, strife (?)

LUDIM, lu'-dim.

LUHITH, lu'-hith, made of tables or boards.

LUKE, luke, light-giving.

LUZ, luz, almond tree.

LYCAONIA, ly-ka-o'-ny-a.

LYCIA, li'-shya, country of the wolf.

LYDIA, lid'-ya, water.

LYDDA, lil'-dah (Greek form of Lud)

LYSANIUS, ly-sa'-ni-us.

LYSIAS, lis'-i-as, dissolving.
LYSTRA, lis'-tra.

MAACHAH, ma'-a-kah, } oppres-
MAACHATHI, ma-ak'-a-thee } sion.
MAACHATHITES, ma-ak'-a-thites, inhabitants of Maachah.
MAADAI, ma-a-da'-i, } ornament
MAADIAH, ma-a-di'-ah, } of Jehovah.
MAAI, ma-a'-i, compassionate.
MAALEH-ACRABBIM, ma'-a-leh-a-crab'-bim, ascent of scorpions.
MAARATH, ma'-a-rath, a place naked of trees.
MAASSEIAH, ma-as-ei'-yah, } work
MAASIAI, ma-as-y-a'-i, } of Jehovah.
MAAZIAH, ma-a-zi'-ah, consolation of Jehovah.
MAATH, ma'-ath, small.
MAAZ, ma'-az, wrath.
MACEDONIA, mas-se-do'-nya.
MACHBANAI, mak-ba-na'-i, what like my sons. Bond of the Lord.
MACHBENAH, mak-be'-nah, bond, cloak.
MACHI, ma'-ki, decrease.
MACHIR, ma'-keer, sold.
MACHNADEBAI, mak-na-de-ba'-i, what is like a liberal person.
MACHPELAH, mak'-pe-lah, a doubling, portion, part, lot.
MADAI, mad'-ai, middle land.
MADIAN, ma'-di-an (see Midian).
MADMANNAH, mad-man'-nah, }
MADMEN, mad'-men, }
MADMENAH, mad-me'-nah, }
dunghill.
MADON, mad'-on, contention.
MAGBISH, mag'-bish, congregating.
MAGDALA, mag'-da-lah, tower.
MAGDALENE, mag'-da-le'-ne or mag'-da-len, inhabitant of Magdala.
MAGDIEL, mag'-di-el, prince of Gog.
MAGOG, ma'-gog, region of God.
MAGOR-MISSABIB, ma'-gor-mis'-sa-bib, fear round about.
MAGPIASH, mag'-pi-ash, killer of moths.
MAHALAH, mah'-ha-lah, disease.
MAHALATH, mah'-ha-lath, a stringed instrument.
MAHALALEEL, ma-ha'-la-lel, praise of God.
MAHALI, mah'-ha-li, sickly.
MAHANAIM, ma-ha-na'-im, camps.

MAHANEH-DAN, mah'-ha-ne-dan', camp of Dan.
MAHARAI, ma-ha-ra'-i, impetuous.
MAHATH, ma'-hath, taking hold, seizing.
MAHAVITE, ma'-ha-vite.
MAHAZIOTH, ma-haz'-i-oth, visions.
MAHER-SHALAL-HASHBAZ, ma'-her-sha'-lal-hash'-baz, hasting to the spoil; he speeds to the prey.
MAHLAH, mah'-lah (see MAHALAH).
MAHOL, ma'-hol, dancing.
MAHLON, mah'-lon, sick.
MAKAZ, ma'-kaz, end.
MAKHELOTH, mak'-he-loth, assemblies, congregations, quoirs.
MAKKEDAH, mak'-ke-dah, of place of shepherds.
MAKTESH, mak'-tesh, mortar.
MALACHI, mal'-a-ki, the messenger of Jehovah.
MALCHAM, mal'-kam, their king.
MALCHIAH, mal-ki'-ah, king of (i. e., appointed by) Jehovah.
MALKIJAH, mal'-ki-jah, k. of (i. e. appointed by) J.
MALCHIEL, mal'-ki-el, k. of (i. e., appointed by) God.
MALCHIRAM, mal-ki'-ram, k. of height.
MALCHISHUA (should be MEL-CHI-SHUAH also), mal-ki-shu'-ah), k. of aid.
MALCHUS, mal'-kus, king, or kingdom.
MALLOTHI, mal-lo'-thi, my fulness.
MALLUK, mal'-luk, reigning, counsellor.
MAMMON, mam'-mon, riches.
MAMRE, mam'-re, fatness, strength.
MANAEN, man'-a-en, their comforter, or leader.
MANAHATH, ma-na'-hath, rest.
MANAHETHITES, ma-na'-heth-ites, inhabitants of Manahath.
MANASSEH, ma-nas'-seh, one who forgets, or makes forget.
MANOAH, ma-no'-ah, rest.
MAOCH, ma'-ok, oppression. A girdle of the breast.
MAON, ma'-on, habitation.
MARA, ma'-ra, sad.
MARAH, ma'-rah, bitter.
MARALAH, mar'-a-lah, trembling, earthquake (?)
MARANATHA, mar-an'-a-thah, the Lord cometh.
MARCUS, mar'-cus, polite, shining.
MARESHAH, ma-re'-shah, that which is at the head.

MARK, mark, polite, shining.

MAROTH, ma'-roth, bitterness, bitter fountains.

MARSENA, mar'-se-na.

MARTHA, mar'-tha, stirring up, bitter, provoking, a lady.

MARY, ma'-ry, rebellion.

MASH, mash, drawn out.

MASHAL, ma'-shal, entreaty.

MASREKAH, mas-re'-kah, vineyard, plantation of noble vines.

MASSA, mas'-sa, lifting up, gift.

MASSAH, mas'-sah, a temptation of Jehovah (or complaining against Him).

MATRED, mat'-red, pushing forward.

MATRI, mat'-ri, vain of Jehovah.

MATTAN, mat'-tan, ⎫ a gift,
MATTANAH, mat'-tan-ah, ⎭ present.

MATTANIAH, mat-tan-i'-ah, ⎫
MATTATHA, ⎬ mat'-ta-thah, ⎱ gift
MATTATHAH, ⎭ ⎰ of Jehovah
MATTATHIAS, mat-ta-thi'-as,
MATTENAI, mat-te-na'-i,

MATTHAN, mat'-than, gift.

MATTHAT, mat'-that, gift of J.

MATTHEW, math'-thew, (contracted from Mattathiah).

MATTHIAS, math-thi'-as, ⎫ gift of
MATTITHIAH, mat-ti-thi'-ah, ⎭ J.

MAZZAROTH, maz'-za-roth, influences; or, prognostications.

MEAH, me'ah, a hundred.

MEARAH, me-a'-rah, cave.

MEBUNNAI, me-bun'-nai, building of Jehovah.

MECHERATHITE, me-ker'-a-thite, inhabitant of Mecherah.

MEDAD, me'-dad, love.

MEDAN, me'-dan, contention.

MEDEBA, me'-de-bah, water of rest.

MEDES, medes, inhabitants of Media.

MEDIA, me'-dya, midst, middle (?)

MEGIDDO, me-gid'-do, ⎫ place of
MEGIDDON, me-gid'-don, ⎭ crowds.

MEHETABEL, ⎫ ⎧whom
⎬me-het'-a-bel,⎨God
MEHETABEEL, ⎭ ⎩benefits.

MEHIDA, me-hi'-da, a joining together.

MEHIR, me'-heer, price.

MEHOLATHITE, me-ho'-lath-ite, native of Meholah.

MEHUJAEL, me-hu'-ja-el, struck by God.

MEHUMAN, me'-hu-man, faithful; also, eunuch.

MEJARKON, me-jar'-kon, waters of yellowness.

MEKONAH, me-ko'-nah, base, foundation.

MELATIAH, me-la-ti'-ah, whom Jehovah freed.

MELCHI, mel'-ki, my king; or, my counsel.

MELCHIAH, mel-ki'-ah, Jehovah's k.

MELCHI-SHUA, mel'-ki-shu'-a, king of aid.

MELCHISEDEK, mel-kiz'-ze-dek, king of righteousness.

MELEA, mel'-e-a, full, fulness.

MELCOM, mel'-kom, thinking.

MELIKU, mel'-i-ku,

MELITA, mel'-i-ta,

MELZAR, mel'-zar, master of wine.

MEMPHIS, mem'-fis, place of (the god) Pthah.

MEMUCAN, mem'-u-kan, dignified (?)

MENAHEM, men'-ha-hem, comforter.

MENAN, me'-nan,

MENI, me-ni', fate, fortune.

MEONENIM, me-on'-e-nim, oak of diviners.

MEONOTHAI, me-on'-o-thai, habitations of Jehovah, my habitations.

MEPHAATH, me-fa'-ath, beauty.

MEPHIBOSHETH, me-fi'-bo-sheth, exterminating the idol.

MERAB, me'-rab, multiplication.

MERAIAH, me-rai'-yah, contumacy (against) Jehovah.

MERAIOTH, me-rai'-yoth, contumacious, rebellious.

MERARI, me-ra'-ri, bitter, unhappy.

MERATHAIM, mer-a-tha'-im, repeated rebellion.

MERCURIUS, mer-cu'-ri-us, or Mercury, the speaker.

MERED, me'-red, rebellion.

MEREMOTH, me-re'-moth, elevations.

MERES, me'-res, lofty.

MERIBAH, me'-ree-bah, water of strife

MERIB-BAAL, me-rib-ba'-al, contender against Baal.

MERODACH, mer'-o-dak, death.

MERODACH-BALADAN, mer'-o-dak-bal'-a-dan, Merodach, worshipper of Bel (?)

MEROM, me'-rom, height, a high place.

MERONOTHITE, me-ron'-o-thite.

MEROZ, me'-roz, refuge.

MESHA, me'-shah, welfare, retreat.

MESHACH, me'-shak, guest of a king.

MESHECH, me'-shek, drawing out.

MESHELEMIAH, me-shel-e-mi'-ah, to whom Jehovah repays (*i.e.*, whom Jehovah treats as a friend).

MESHEZABEEL, me-she'-za-bel, whom God frees.

MESHILLEMITH, me-shil'-le-mith, } MESHILLEMOTH, me-shil'-le-moth, } those who repay.

MESHOBAB, me-sho'-bab, brought back.

MESHULLAM, me-shul'-lam, friend (of God).

MESHULLEMETH, me-shul'-le-meth, friend (fem.) of God.

MESOBAITE, me-so'-ba-ite, inhabitant of Mesoba.

MESOPOTAMIA, mes-o-po-ta'-mi-a, amidst the rivers.

MESSIAH, mes-si'-ah, anointed.

METHEG-AMMAH, me'-theg-am'-mah, bridle of the metropolis.

METHUSAEL, me-thu'-sa-el, man of God.

METHUSELAH, me-thu'-se-lah, man of a dart.

MEUNIM, me-u'-nim, habitations.

MEZAHAB, me'-za-hab, water (*i.e.*, splendour) of gold.

MIAMIN, mi'-a-min, from the right hand.

MIBHAR, mib'-har, choicest.

MIBSAM, mib'-sam, sweet odour.

MIBZAR, mib'-zar, a fortress.

MICAH, mi'-kah, } who (is) like MICAIAH, mi-kai'-yah } unto Jehovah.

MICHAEL, mi'-ka-el, } who (is) like MICHAL, mi'-kal, } unto God?

MICHMAS, mik'-mas } laid up, MICHMASH, mik'-mash, } treasure.

MICHMETHAH, mik'-me-thah, hiding place.

MICHRI, mik'-ri, worthy of price, price of Jehovah.

MIDDIN, mid'-din, measures.

MIDIAN, mid'-yan, strife.

MIDIANITES, mid'-yan-ites, people of Midian.

MIGDALEL, mig'-da-lel, tower of God.

MIGDAL-GAD, mig'-dal-gad, t. of Gad.

MIGDOL, mig'-dol, tower?

MIGRON, mig'-ron, a precipitous place.

MIJAMIN, mi'-ja-min, from the right hand.

MIKLOTH, mik'-loth, staves, lots.

MIKNEIAH, mik-nei'-yah, possession of Jehovah.

MILALAI, mil-al-a'-i, eloquent.

MILCAH, mil'-kah, counsel.

MILCOM, mil'-kom, great king.

MILETUM, mi-le'-tum, improper form of Miletus.

MILETUS, mi-le'-tus.

MILLO, mil'-lo, a rampart, mound.

MINIAMIN, min'-ya-min, from the right hand.

MINNI, min' i, division.

MINNITH, min'-nith, allotment.

MIRIAM, mir'-ri-am, their contumacy

MIRMA, meer'-ma, fraud.

MISGAB, mis'-gab, height.

MISHAEL, mi'-sha-el, who is what God is (?)

MISHAL, mish'-al, } prayer. MISHAL, mish'-i-al, }

MISHAM, mish'-am, their cleansing.

MISHMA, mish'-ma, a hearing.

MISHMANNAH, mish-man'-nah, fatness.

MISHRAITES, mish'-ra-ites.

MISPAR, mis'-par, number.

MISPERETH, mis'-pe-reth.

MISREPHOTH-MAIM, mis'-re-foth-ma'-im, the flow of waters.

MITHCAH, mith-kah, sweetness (probably sweet fountain.)

MITHNITE, mith'-nite.

MITHREDATH, mith'-re-dath, given by Mithras.

MITYLENE, mit-y-le'-ne.

MIZAR, mi'-zar, smallness.

MIZPAH, miz'-pah, } watch-tower, MIZPEH, miz'-peh, } lofty place.

MIZRAIM, miz'-ra-im, bulwarks, fortresses.

MIZZAH, miz'-zah, fear, trepidation.

MNASON, na'-son, a diligent seeker, a remembrancer.

MOAB, mo'-ab, progeny of a father.

MOABITES, mo'-ab-ites, people of Moab.

MOADIAH, mo-a-di'-ah, festival of Jehovah.

MOLADAH, mo'-la-dah, birth, race.

MOLECH, mo'-lek, } king. MOLOCH, mo-lok, }

MOLID, mo'-lid, begetter.

MORASTHITE, mo-ras'-thite, native of Moresheth.

MORDECAI, mor'-de-kai, little man, or worshipper of Mars.

MOREH, mo'-reh, the hill of the teacher.

MORESHETH-GATH, mo'-re-sheth-gath, the possession of the Gittites.

MORIAH, mo-ri'-ah, chosen by J.

MOSERA, mo'-se-rah, bonds.

MOSEROTH, mo'-se-roth, bond.

MOSES, mo'-zez, drawn out, saved from the water.

MOZA, mo'-za, } fountain.
MOZAR, mo'-zah, }

MUPPIM, mup'-pim (probably same as Shupham, q. v.)

MUSHI, mu'-shi, yielding, proved by Jehovah.

MUTHLABBEN, muth-lab'-ben, chorus of virgins (?)

MYRA, my'-rah.

MYSIA, mish'-ya,

NAAM, na'-am, pleasantness.

NAAMITES, na'-am-ites (named from the foregoing [?]).

NAAMAH, na'-a-mah, } pleasant.
NAAMAN, na'-a-man, }

NAAMATHITE, na-am'-ath-ite, descendant of Naaman.

NAARAH, na'-a-rah, }
NAARAI, na'-a-ra'-i, } a girl, handmaid.
NAARATH, na'-a-rath, }

NAARAN, na'-a-ran, juvenile, puerile.

NAASHON, na-ash'-on, } enchanter.
NAASSON, na-as'-son, }

NABAL, na'-bal, foolish.

NABOTH, na'-both, fruit, produce.

NACHON, na'-kon, prepared.

NACHOR, na'-kor (see NAHOR).

NADAB, na'-dab, spontaneous, liberal.

NAGGE, nag'-ge, illuminating.

NAHALIEL, na-ha'-li-el, valley of God.

NAHALLAL, nah'-al-al, } pasture.
NAHALOL, nah'-al-ol, }

NAHAM, na'-ham, consolation.

NAHAMANI, na-ha-ma'-ni, repenting, merciful.

NAHARAI, na'-ha-rai, snorter.

NAHASH, na'-hash, serpent.

NAHATH, na'-hath, rest.

NAHBI, nah'-bi, hidden.

NAHOR, na'-hor, breathing hard, snorting.

NAHUM, na'-hum, comfort, consolation.

NAHSHON, nah'-shon, enchanter.

NAIN, na'-in, pleasant.

NAIOTH, nai'-yoth, habitations.

NAOMI, na'-o-mi, my pleasantness.

NAPHISH, na'-fish, refreshment.

NAPHTALI, naf'-ta-li, my strife.

NAPHTUHIM, naf'-tu-him, border-people.

NARCISSUS, nar-sis'-sus, stupidity, surprise.

NATHAN, na'-than, whom God gave.

NATHANAEL, na-than'-a-el, whom God gave.

NATHAN-MELECH, na'-than-me'-lek, whom the king has placed.

NAUM, na'-um, consolation.

NAZARENES, naz-a-reens', natives of Nazareth.

NAZARETH, naz'-a-reth, separated.

NAZARITE, naz'-a-rite, one separated.

NEAH, ne'-ah, shaking, perhaps of the earth.

NEAPOLIS, ne-ap'-po-lis, new city.

NEARIAH, ne-a-ri'-ah, servant of Jehovah.

NEBAI, ne-ba'-i, fruit-bearing.

NEBAIOTH, ne-bai'-yoth, } high
NEBAJOTH, ne-ba'-joth, } places.

NEBALLAT, ne-bal'-lat, folly, or wickedness, in secret.

NEBAT, ne'-bat, aspect.

NEBO, ne'-bo, interpreter.

NEBUCHAD- } neb'-u-kad- } the
NEZZAR, } nez'-zar, } prince
NEBUCHAD- } neb'-u-kad- } of the
REZZAR, } rez'-zar, } god Nebo.

NEBUSHASBAN, neb-u-shas'-ban, worshipper of Nebo.

NEBUZAR-ADAN, neb-u-zar'-a-dan, leader whom Nebo favours.

NECHO, } ne'-ko, lame.
NICHOH, }

NEDABIAH, ned-a-bi'-ah, whom Jehovah impels.

NEGINAH, neg'-ee-nah, a stringed instrument.

NEGINOTH, neg'-ee-noth, stringed instruments.

NEHELAMITE, ne-hel'-a-mite,

NEHEMIAH, ne-he-mi'-ah, whom Jehovah comforts.

NEHUM, ne'-hum, consolation (qy. an error for Rehum?).

NEHUSHTA, ne-hush'-ta, } brass.
NEHUSHTAH, ne-hush'-tah, }

NEHUSHTAN, ne-hush'-tan, brazen.

NEIEL, nei'-yel, moved by God.

NEKEB, ne'-keb, carrion.

NEKODA, ne-ko'-dah, distinguished.

NEMUEL, nem'-u-el, day of God.

NEMUELITES, ne-mu'-el-ites, descendants of Nemuel.

NEPHEG, ne'-feg, sprout.

NEPHTHALIM, nef'-ta-lim (see NAPHTALI), my strife.

NEPHTOAH, nef-to'-ah, opening.

NEPHISH, ne'-fish, refreshed.

NEPHISHESIM, ne-fish'-e-sim, }
NEPHUSIM, nef'-u-sim, } expansions.

NER, ner, light, lamp.

NEREUS, ne'-reus, a candle, light.

NERGAL, ner'-gal, devourer of man, hero.

NERGAL-SHAREZER, ner'-gal-sha-re'-zer

NETHANAEL (see NATHANAEL).

NETHANIAH, neth-a-ni'-ah, whom Jehovah gave.

NETHINIM, neth'-in-im, the devoted.

NERIAH, ne'-ri-ah, lamp of Jehovah.

NETOPHAH, ne-to'-fah, a dropping.

NETOPHATHITES, ne-to'-fa-thites, inhabitants of Netophah.

NEZIAH, ne-zi'-ah, pure, sincere.

NEZIB, ne'-zib, garrison, statue.

NIBHAZ, nib'-haz, barker (?)

NIBSHAN, nib'-shan, soft soil.

NICANOR, ni-ka'-nor, a conqueror.

NICODEMUS, nik-o-de'-mus, innocent blood; conqueror of the people.

NICOLAITANES, nik-o-la'-i-tanes, named after Nicolas.

NICOLAS, nik'-o-las, conquering the people.

NICOPOLIS, ni-kop'-o-lis, a city of victory.

NIGER, ni'-jer, black.

NIMRAH, nim'-rah, } limpid (water).
NIMRIM, nim'-rim, }

NIMROD, nim'-rod, rebel.

NIMSHI, nim'-shi, drawn out.

NINEVEH, nin'-e-veh, dwelling of Ninus (?)

NISROCH, niz'-rok, eagle, great eagle.

No, no, } portion or
NO-A-MON, no-a'-mon, } temple of Amon.

NOADIAH, no-a-di'-ah, with whom Jehovah meets.

NOAH, no'-ah, rest, motion.

NOB, nob, high place.

NOBAH, no'-bah, a barking.

NOD, nod, flight, wandering.

NODAB, no'-dab, nobility.

NOGAH, no'-gah, brightness.

NOHAH, no'-hah, rest.

NON, non, fish.

NOPH, noff, (same as MEMPHIS, q. v.)

NOPHAH, no'-phah, blast; perhaps a place through which the wind blows.)

NUN, nun, fish.

NYMPHAS, nim'-fas, bridegroom.

OBADIAH, o-ba-di'-ah, worshipper of Jehovah.

OBAL, o'-bal, stripped, bare of leaves.

OBED, o'-bed, worshipping (God).

OBEDEDOM, o-bed-e'-dom, he who serves the Edomites.

OBIT, o'-bit, one who is set over camels.

OBOTH, o'-both, bottles (of skin).

OCRAN, ok'-ran, troubled.

ODED, o'-ded, restoring, setting-up.

OG, og, in stature, long-necked, gigantic.

OHAD, o'-had, united.

OHEL, o'-hel, tent.

OLIVET, ol'-i-vet, place of olives.

OLYMPAS, o-lim'-pas, heavenly.

OMAR, o'-mar, eloquent, talkative.

OMEGA, o'-meg-a, great O.

OMRI, om'-ri, servant of Jehovah, perhaps young learner of Jehovah; unskilful.

ON, on, light, especially the sun; strength.

ONAM, o'-nam, strong.

ONAN, o'-nan,

ONESIMUS, o-ne'-si-mus, profitable, useful.

ONESIPHORUS, o-ne-sif'-o-rus, bringing profit.

ONO, o'-no, strong.

OPHEL, o'-fel, a hill, an acclivity.

OPHIR, o'-feer, abundance.

OPHNI, off'-ni, mouldy.

OPHRAH, off'-rah, fawn.

OREB, o'-reb, raven.

OREN, o'-ren, pine-tree.

ORION, o-ri'-on, the giant.

ORNAN, or'-nan, nimble.

ORPAH, or'-pah, mane, forelock, kind.

OSEAS, o-ze'-as, or OSEE, o'-zee, (see HOSEA).

OSHEA, o-she'-a, (see JOSHUA).

OTHNI, oth'-ni, lion of Jehovah.

OTHNIEL, oth'-ni-el, lion of God.

OZEM, o'-zem, strong.

OZIAS, o-zi'-as (see UZZIAH).

OZNI, oz'-ni, hearing.

OZNITES, oz'-nites, descendants of Ozni.

PAARAI, pa-a-rai, (probably same as NAARAI, q.v.)

PADAN-ARAM, pa'-dan-a'-ram, the plain of Syria.

PADON, pa'-don, liberation, redemption.

PAGIEL, pa'-gi-el, fortune of God.

PAHATH-MOAB, pa'-hath-mo'-ab, governor of Moab.

PAI, pa'-i, bleating.

PALAL, pa'-lal, judge.

PALESTINA, pal-es-ti'-na, land of strangers.

PALLU, pal'-lu, distinguished.

PALLUITES, pal'-lu-ites, descendants of Pallu.

PALTI, pal'-ti, deliverance of Jehovah.

PALTIEL, pal'-ti-el, deliverance of J.

PAMPHYLIA, pam-fil'-i-a.

PAPHOS, pa'-fos.

PARAH, pa'-rah, village of heifers.

PARAN, pa'-ran, a region abounding in foliage, or in caverns.

PARBAR, par'-bar, open apartment.

PARMASHTA, par-mash'-ta, strong-fisted, superior.

PARMENAS, par'-me-nas, abiding.

PARNACH, par'-nak, delicate.

PAROSH, pa'-rosh, flea.

PARSHANDATHA, par-shan-da'-tha, given forth to light.

PARTHIANS, par'-thi-ans,

PARUAH, par-u'-ah, flourishing.

PARVAIM, par-va'-im, oriental regions

PASACH, pa'-sak, cut off.

PASDAMMIN, pas-dam'-min, boundary of blood.

PASEAH, pa-se'-ah, lame, limping.

PASHUR, pash'-ur, prosperity everywhere.

PATARA, pat'-a-rah.

PATHROS, path'-ros, region of the south.

PATHRUSIM, path-ru'-sim, people of Pathros.

PATMOS, pat'-mos,

PATROBAS, pat'-ro-bas, paternal.

PAU, pa'-u, bleating.

PAUL, pawl, little.

PEDAHEL, ped'-a-hel, whom God preserved, redeemed.

PEDAHZUR, ped-ah'-zur, whom the rock (i. e., God) preserved.

PEDAIAH, pe-dai'-yah, whom Jehovah preserved, redeemed.

PEKAH, pe'-kah, open-eyed.

PEKAHIAH, pe-ka-hi'-ah, whose eyes Jehovah opened.

PEKOD, pe'-kod, visitation.

PELAIAH, pel-ai'-yah, whom Jehovah made distinguished.

PELALIAH, pel-a-li'-ah, whom J. judged.

PELATIAH, pel-a-ti'-ah, whom J. delivered.

PELEG, pe'-leg, division, part.

PELET, pe'-let, liberation.

PELETH, pe'-leth, swiftness.

PELETHITES, pel'-leth-ites, runners.

PELONITE, pel'-o-nite,

PENIEL, pen-ee'-el, the face of God.

PENINNAH, pe-nin'-nah, coral, pearl.

PENTECOST, pen'-te-kost, fiftieth.

PENUEL, pe-nu'-el, (see PENIEL).

PEOR, pe'-or, hiatus, cleft.

PERAZIM, pe-ra'-zim, breaches.

PERESH, pe'-resh, dung.

PEREZ, pe'-rez, breach.

PEREZ-UZZA, pe'-rez-uz'-zah, b. of Uzzah.

PERGA, per'-gah.

PERGAMOS, per'-ga-mos,

PERIDA, pe-ri'-dah, grain, kernel.

PERIZZITES, per'-iz-zites, belonging to a village.

PERSIA, per'-shya.

PERSIAN, per'-shyan, belonging to Persia.

PERUDA, pe-ru'-dah (see PERIDA).

PETER, pe'-ter, a rock or stone.

PETHAHIAH, peth-a-hi'-ah, whom Jehovah looses, i. e., sets free.

PETHOR, pe'-thor, interpreter of dreams.

PETHUEL, pe-thu'-el, vision of God.

PEULTHAI, pe-ul'-thai, wages of J.

PHALEC, fa'-lek, (see PELEG).

PHALTI, fal'-ti, deliverance of J.

PHANUEL, fa'-nu-el, face, or vision of God.

PHARAOH, fa'-roh, the sun (Phrah).

PHARAOH-NECHOH, fa'-ro-ne'-ko, Phrah or Pharaoh the lame.

PHAREZ, fa'-rez, breach.

PHARISEES, fa'-ri-sees, the separated.

PHARPAR, far'-par, swift.

PHASEAH, fa-ze'-ah, lame, limping.

PHEBE, fe'-be, shining, pure.

PHENICE, fe-ni'-se, } land of
PHENICIA, fe-nish'-ya, } palms.

PHICOL, fi'-kol, the mouth of all (commanding all).

PHILADELPHIA, fil-a-del'-fi-a, brotherly love.

PHILEMON, fi-le'-mon, affectionate, kisser.

PHILETUS, fi-le'-tus, beloved, amiable.

PHILIP, fil'-lip, warlike, lover of horses.

PHILIPPI, fil-lip'-pi, belonging to Philip.

PHILIPPIANS, fil-lip'-pi-ans, the people of Philippi.

PHILISTIA, fil-lis'-ti-a, the land of wanderers, strangers.

PHILISTIM, fil-lis'-tim, } wan-
PHILISTINES, fil-lis'-tines, } derers.

PHILOLOGUS, fil-lol'-lo-gus, a lover of learning, a lover of the word.

PHINEHAS, fin'-e-as, mouth of brass.

PHLEGON, fle'-gon, zealous, burning.

PHRYGIA, frij'-ya,

PHURAH, fu'-rah, branch.

PHUT, fut, afflicted, a bow.

PHYGELLUS, fi-gel'-lus, little, fugitive.

PI-BESETH, pi-be'-seth, words of Pasht (?)

PIHAHIROTH, pi-ha-hi'-roth, where grass or rush grows.

PILATE, pi'-lat,

PILEHAH, pil-e'-hah, a slice.

PINON, pi'-non, darkness.

PIRAM, pi'-ram, like a wild ass, perhaps in running.

PIRATHON, pir'-a-thon, prince.

PIRATHONITE, pi'-ra-thon-ite.

PILDASH, pil'-dash, flame.

PILTAI, pil'-tai, whom J. delivers.

PISGAH, piz'-gah, a part, a fragment.

PISIDIA, pi-sid'-i-a.

PISON, pi'-son, water poured forth, overflowing.

PISPAH, pis'-pah, dispersion.

PITHOM, pi'-thom, narrow place.

PITHON, pi'-thon.

PLEIADES, pli'-a-deez, a heap, cluster.

POCHERETH OF ZEBAIM, po'-ke-reth of Ze-ba'-im, snaring gazelles.

POLLUX, pol'-lux.

PONTIUS, pon'-ti-us.

PONTUS, pon'-tus, sea.

PORATHA, po-ra'-thah, given by lot.

PORCIUS-FESTUS, por'-shi-us-fes'-tus

POTIPHAR, pot'-i-far, } De-
POTIPHERAH, pot-i-fe'-rah, } longing to the sun (Phrah).

PRISCILLA, pris-sil'-lah, ancient.

PROCHORUS, prok'-o-rus, he tha'. presides over the choir.

PTOLEMAIS, tol-e-ma'-is, city of Ptolemy.

PUAH, pu'-ah, mouth, splendid.

PUBLIUS, pub'-li-us, common.

PUDENS, pu'-dens, shamefaced.

PUHITES, pu'-hites.

PUL, pul, elephant, lord.

PUNITES, pu'-nites, descendants of Pun.

PUNON, pu'-non, darkness, obscurity.

PUR, pur, } a lot.
PURIM, pu'-rim, } lots.

PUT, put, afflicted.

PUTIEL, pu'-ti-el, afflicted by God.

PUTEOLI, pu-te'-o-li.

QUARTUS, kwar'-tus, the fourth.

RAAMAH, ra'-a-mah, trembling.

RAAMIAH, ra-a-mi'-ah, whom Jehovah makes to tremble (who fears J.).

RAAMSES, ra-am'-ses, son of the sun.

RABBAH, rab'-bah, } capital city.
RABBATH, rab'-bath, }

RABBI, rab'-bi, master.

RABBITH, rab'-bith, multitude.

RABBONI, rab-bo'-ni, my master.

RABMAG, rab'-mag, prince of magi.

RABSARIS, rab'-sa-ris, chief eunuch.

RABSHAKEH, rab'-sha-keh, chief of the cupbearers.

RACHAL, ra'-cal, traffic.

RACHEL, ra'-chel, ewe.

RADDAI, rad'-dai, subduing.

RAGAU, ra'-gaw, (see REU).

RAGUEL, rag'-u-el, friend of God.

RAHAB, ra'-hab, gracious.

RAHAM, ra'-ham, womb.

RAHEL, ra'-hel, (see RACHEL).

RAKEM, ra'-kem, variegation, flower-garden.

RAKKATH, rak'-kath, shore.

RAKKON, rak'-kon, thinness.

RAM, ram, high.

RAMAH, ra'-mah, } high place.
RAMATH, ra'-math, }

RAMATHAIM, ra-math-a'-im, double high place.

RAMATH-LEHI, ra'-math-le'-hi height of Lehi

RAMATH-MISPEH, ra'-math-mis'-peh, height of Mizpeh.

RAMESES, ram'-e-seez, son of the sun.

RAMIAH, ra-mi'-ah, whom J. set.

RAMOTH, ra'-moth, high things, heights; figuratively, sublime, difficult things.

RAMOTH-GILEAD, ra'-moth-gil'-e-ad, h. of Gilead.

RAPHU, ra'-fu, healed.

REAIA, REAIAH, } re-ai'-yah, { whom Jehovah cares for.

REBA, re'-ba, a fourth part.

REBECCA, REBEKAH, } re-bek'-ah, { a rope with a noose.

RECHAB, re'-kab, horseman.

RECHABITES, re'-kab-ites, descendants of Rechab.

RECHAH, re'-kah, side, utmost part.

REELAIAH, re-el-ai'-yah, whom Jehovah makes to tremble (who fears J.).

REGEM, re'-gem, friend (of God).

REGEM-MELECH, re'-gem-me'-lek, f. of the king.

REHABIAH, re-ha-bi'-ah, for whom Jehovah makes an ample space.

REHOB, re'-hob, street.

REHOBOAM, re-ho-bo'-am, who enlarges the people.

REHOBOTH, re-ho'-both, streets, wide spaces.

REHUM, re'-hum, beloved, merciful.

REI, re'-i, companionable.

REKEM, re'-kem, flower-garden, variegated.

REMALIAH, rem-a-li'-ah, whom Jehovah adorned.

REMETH, re'-meth, a high place.

REMMON, rem'-mon, (see RIMMON).

REMPHAN, rem'-fan, frame, model (?)

REPHAEL, re'-fa-el, whom God healed

REPHAH, re'-fah, riches.

REFAIAH, ref-ai'-yah, whom J. healed.

REPHAIM, re-fa'-im, } giants, REPHAIMS, re-fa'-ims, } chiefs (?)

REPHIDIM, ref'-i-dim, props, supports.

RESEN, re'-sen, bridle.

RESHEF, re'-shef, flame.

REU, re'-u, friend (of God).

REUBEN, rew'-ben, (behold, a son ?)

REUBENITES, rew'-ben-ites, descendants of Reuben.

REUEL, rew'-el, friend of God.

REUMAH, re-ew'-mah, exalted.

REZEPH, re'-zef, a stone (used for culinary purposes)

REZIA, rez'-i-a, delight.

REZIN, re'-zin, firm, stable, a prince.

REZON, re'-zon, prince.

RHEGIUM, re'-ji-um, a breaking.

RHESA, re'-sah, affection, a heart.

RHODA, ro'-da, } a rose. RHODES, rodes, }

RIBAI, ri'-bai, whose cause J. pleads.

RIBLAH, rib'-lah, fertility.

RIMMON, rim'-mon, the exalted, pomegranate.

RIMMON-PAREZ, rim'-mon-pa'-rez, p. of the breach.

RIMNAH, rim'-nah, shout.

RIPHATH, ri'-fath, shout.

RISSAH, ris'-sah, dew, full of dew, ruin.

RIZPAH, riz'-pah, coal, hot stone.

RITHMAH, rith'-mah, genista, or broom.

ROBOAM, ro-bo'-am, (see REHOBOAM).

ROGELIM, ro'-ge-lim, place of fullers.

ROHGAH, ro'-gah, outcry.

ROMAM-TIEZER, ro-mam'-ti-e'-zer, whose help I have exalted.

ROMANS, ro'-mans, men of Rome.

ROME, rome, (generally derived from Romulus, the supposed founder).

ROSH, rosh, bear, chief.

RUFUS, ru'-fus, red.

RUHAMAH, ru'-ha-mah, compassionated.

RUMAH, ru'-mah, high.

RUTH, rooth, appearance, beauty.

SABACTHANI, sa-bak'-tha-nee, thou hast forsaken me.

SABAOTH, sab-a'-oth, hosts.

SABEANS, sa-be'-ans, descendants of Saba.

SABTAH, sab'-tah, striking.

SABTEKAH, sab'-te-kah.

SACAR, sa'-car, hire, reward.

SADDUCEES, sad'-du-seez, named from Zadok.

SADOK, sa'-dok, just.

SALAH, sa'-lah, shoot, sprout.

SALAMIS, sal'-a-mis,

SALATHIEL, sa-la'-thi-el, whom I asked for from God.

SALCAH, sal'-cah, pilgrimage.

SALEM, sa'-lem, } peace. SALIM, sa'-lim, }

SALLAI, sal'-lai, lifted up, basket weaver.

SALLU, sal'-lu, weighed.

SALMA, sal'-ma, } garment.
SALMAH, sal'-mah, } garment.
SALMON, sal'-mon, clothed.
SALMONE, sal-mo'-ne.
SALOME, sa-lo'-me, peaceable, perfect, reward.
SALU, sa'-lu, (see SALLU).
SAMARIA, sa-ma'-ri-a, pertaining to a watch, watch-mountain.
SAMARITANS, sa-mar'-i-tans, inhabitants of Samaria.
SAMGAR-NEBO, sam'-gar-no'-bo, sword of Nebo.
SAMLAH, sam'-lah, garment.
SAMOS, sa'-mos.
SAMOTHRACIA, sam-o-thra'-shya.

SAMSON, sam'-son, solar, like the sun.
SAMUEL, sam'-u-el, heard of God, name of God.
SANBALLAT, san-bal'-lat, praised by the army.
SANHEDRIM, san'-he-drim.
SANSANNAH, san-san'-nah, palm branch.
SAPH, saff, threshold, tall (?)
SAPHIR, sa'-feer, } beautiful.
SAPPHIRA, saf-fi'-ra, } beautiful.
SARAH, sa'-rah, abundance, princess.
SARAI, sa'-rai, my princess, nobility.
SARAPH, sa'-raf, burning, venomous.
SARDIS, sar'-dis.
SARDITES, sard'-ites, descendants of Sered.
SAREPTA, sa-rep'-tah, (see ZAREPHATH).
SARGON, sar'-gon, prince of the sun.
SARID, sa'-rid, survivor.
SARSECHIM, sar'-se-kim, chief of the eunuchs.
SARUCH, sa'-ruk, (see SERUG).
SATAN, sa'-tan, adversary.
SAUL, sawl, asked for.
SCEVA, se'-vah, disposed, prepared.
SCYTHIAN, sith'-i-an.
SEBA, se'-ba, man (?)
SEBAT, se'-bat, sprout (?)
SECACAH, sek-a'-kah, enclosure.
SECHU, se'-ku, hill, watch-tower.
SECUNDUS, se'-kun-dus, second.
SEGUB, se'-gub.
SEIR, se'-ir, } hairy, rough.
SEIRATH, se-i'-rath, } hairy, rough.
SELA, se'-lah, rock.
SELA-HAMMAHLEKOTH, se'-lah-ham-mah'-le-koth, r. of escapes.

SELAH, se'-lah (probably a musical direction).
SELED, se'-led, exultation, or burning.
SELEUCIA, se-lew'-shya.
SEMACHIAH, sem-a-ki'-ah, whom Jehovah sustains.
SEMEI, sem'-e-i, renowned.
SENAAH, se-na'-ah, perhaps thorny.
SENEH, sen'-eh, crag, thorn, rock.
SENIR, se'-neer, coat of mail, cataract.
SENNACHERIB, sen-nak'-e-rib, conqueror of armies.
SENUAH, se-nu'-ah, hated.
SEORIM, se-o'-rim, barley.
SEPHAR, se'-far, a numbering.
SEPHARAD, sef-a'-rad,
SEPHARVAIM, sef-ar-va'-im, the two Sipparas.
SERAH, se'-rah, abundance, princess.
SERAIAH, ser-ai'-yah, soldier of J.
SERAPHIM, ser'-ra-fim, lofty ones.
SERED, se'-red, fear.
SERGIUS, ser'-ji-us.
SERUG, se'-rug, shoot.
SETH, seth, placing, setting in the stead of another.
SETHUR, se'-thur, hidden.
SHAALABBIN, sha-al-ab'-bin, } place of foxes, or jackals.
SHAALBIM, sha-al'-bim, } place of foxes, or jackals.
SHAALBONITE, sha-al'-bon-ite, inhabitant of Shaalbim.
SHAAPH, sha'-aff, division.
SHAARAIM, sha-ar-a'-im, two gates.
SHAHARAIM, sha-har-a'-im, two dawns.
SHAASHGAZ, sha-ash'-gaz, beauty's servant.
SHABBETHAI, shab-beth-a'-i, born on the sabbath.
SHACHIA, shak'-i-a, wandering.
SHADRACH, sha'-drak, rejoicing on the way.
SHAGE, sha'-ge, wandering.
SHAHAZIMAH, sha-haz-i'-mah, lofty places.
SHALEM, sha'-lem, safe, principal
SHALLECHETH, shal-le'-keth, casting down.
SHALIM, sha'-lim, region of foxes.
SHALISHA, shal'-i-sha, triangular.
SHALLUM, shal'-lum, } retribution.
SHALLUN, shal'-lun, } retribution.
SHALMAI, shal'-mai, my thanks.
SHALMAN, shal'-man,
SHALMANESER, shal-ma-ne'-zer, worshipper of fire.

SHAMARIAH, sham-a-ri'-ah, whom Jehovah guards.

SHAMA, sha'-ma, hearing, obedient.

SHAMED, sha'-med, destroyer.

SHAMER, sha'-mer, keeper.

SHAMGAR, sham'-gar, warrior (?)

SHAMHUTH, sham'-huth, desolation.

SHAMIR, sha'-mir, a sharp point, thorn.

SHAMMA, sham'-mah, desert.

SHAMMAH, sham'-mah, astonishment.

SHAMMAI, sham'-mai, laid waste.

SHAMMOTH, sham'-moth, desolation.

SHAMMUA, } sham-mu'-ah, rumour.
SHAMMUAH, }

SHAMSHERAI, sham-she-ra'-i.

SHAPHAM, sha'-fam, bald, shaven.

SHAPHAN, sha'-fan, coney.

SHAPHAT, sha'-phat, judge.

SHAPHER, sha'-pher, pleasantness.

SHARAI, sha-ra'-i, whom J. frees.

SHARAIM, sha-ra'-im, two gates.

SHARAR, sha'-rar, twisted, a cord, muscular.

SHAREZER, sha-re'-zer, prince of fire.

SHARON, sha'-ron, plain, plain country

SHARUHEN, sha-ru'-hen, pleasant lodging place.

SHASHAI, sha'-shai, whitish.

SHASHAK, sha'-shak, desire.

SHAVEH, sha'-veh, plain.

SHAVEH-KIRIATHAIM, sha'veh-kir-ya-tha'-im, p. of Kiriathaim

SHAUL, shawl, asked for.

SHAULITES, shawl'-ites,

SHEAL, she'-al, prayer.

SHEALTIEL, she-al'-ti-el, whom I asked for from God.

SHEBARIAH, she-ar-i'-ah, whom Jehovah estimates.

SHEAR-JASHUB, she'-ar-ja'-shub, a remnant shall return.

SHEBAH, } she'-bah, man, scorn, or
SHEBA, } au oath.

SHEBAM, she'-bam, coolness, sweet smell.

SHEBANIAH, she-ba-ni'-ah, whom J. made to grow up.

SHEBARIM, she-ba'-rim, breaches.

SHEBER, she'-ber, breaking.

SHEBNA, sheb'-nah, tender youth, youth.

SHEBUEL, she-bu'-el, captive of God.

SHECANIAH, shek-a-ni'-ah, intimate with Jehovah, as if dwelling with Him.

SHECHEM, shek'-em, back, shield, or blade.

SHECHEMITES, shek'-em-ites, people of Shechem

SHEDEUR, shed-e'-ur, casting forth of fire.

SHEHARIAH, she-ha-ri'-ah, whom Jehovah seeks for.

SHELAH, she'-lah, petition.

SHELEMIAH, shel-e-mi'-ah, whom Jehovah repays.

SHELEF, she'-lef, drawn out, saluted.

SHELESH, she'-lesh, triad.

SHELOMI, she-lo'-mi, } peaceful,
SHELOMITH, shel-o'-mith, } love of peace.

SHELUMIEL, she-lu'-mi-el, friend of God.

SHEM, shem, name.

SHEMA, she'-ma, } rumour.
SHEMAAH, she-ma'-ah, }

SHEMAIAH, shem-ai'-yah, whom Jehovah has heard and answered.

SHEMARIAH, shem-a-ri'-ah, whom Jehovah guards.

SHEMEBER, shem-e'-ber, soaring on high.

SHEMER, she'-mer, guardian.

SHEMIDA, she-mi'-da, fame of wisdom

SHEMINITH, she-mee'-nith, eighth.

SHEMIRAMOTH, she-mir'-a-moth, most high name, or most high heaven.

SHEMUEL, shem'-u-el, heard of God, name of God.

SHEN, shen, truth.

SHENAZAR, she-na'-zar, fiery.

SHENER, she'-ner, coat of mail, cataract.

SHEPHAM, she'-fam, nakedness, a place naked of trees.

SHEPHATIAH, shep-a-ti'-ah, whom Jehovah defends.

SHEPHI, she'-fi, naked hill.

SHEPHO, she'-fo, nakedness,

SHEPHUPHAN, she-fu'-fan, serpent, cerastes, or horned snake.

SHERAH, she'-rah, consanguinity.

SHEREBIAH, sher-e-bi'-ah, heat of J.

SHERESH, she'-resh, root.

SHESHACH, she'-shak, moon god (?)

SHESHAI, she'-shai, whitish (?)

SHESHAN, she'-shan, lily.

SHESHBAZZAR, shesh-baz'-zar, fire worshipper.

SHETHAR, she'-thar, star.

SHETHAR-BOZNAI, she'-thar-boz'-nai bright star.

SHEVA, she'-va, hesitation.

SHIBBOLETH, shib'-bo-leth, flood.
SHIBMAH, shib'-mah, coolness, or sweet smell.
SHICRON, shik'-ron, drunkenness.
SHIGGAION, shig-gai'-yon, } erratic
SHIGIONOTH, shig'-yo-noth, } wandering.
SHIHON, shi'-hon, overturning.
SHIHOR-LIBNAH, shi'-hor-lib'-nah, } black river
SHIHOR-LIBNATH, shi'-hor-lib'-nath, } of glass.
SHILHIM, shil'-him, armed men.
SHILLEM, shil'-lem, requital.
SHILOAH, shi-lo'-ah, sending (of water by a conduit).
SHILOH, shi'-lo, place of rest.
SHILONI, shi-lo'-ni, pacificator.
SHILONITE, shi'-lo-nite, native of Shiloh.
SHILSAH, shil'-shah, triad.
SHIMEA, shim'-e-ah,
SHIMEAH, shim'-e-ah } rumour, fame.
SHIMEAM, shim'-e-am,
SHIMEI, shim'-e-i, } rumour,
SHIMEATH, shim'-e-ath, } famous, renowned.
SHIMHI, shim'-hi, renowned.
SHIMEON, shim'-e-on, a hearkening.
SHIMMA, shim'-ma, rumour.
SHIMON, shi'-mon, desert.
SHIMRATH, shim'-rath, watch.
SHIMRI, shim'-ri, watchful.
SHIMRITH, shim'-rith, vigilant.
SHIMROM, shim'-rom, } watch-post.
SHIMRON, shim'-ron,
SHIMRONITES, shim'-ron-ites, descendants of Shimron.
SHIMSHAI, shim'-shai, sunny.
SHINAB, shi'-nab, father's tooth.
SHINAR, shi'-nar, casting out (?), land of two rivers (!)
SHIPHI, shi'-fi, abundant.
SHIPHRAH, shif'-rah, beauty.
SHIPHTAN, shif'-tan, judicial.
SHISHA, shi'-sha, habitation.
SHISHAK, shi'-shak.
SHITRAI, shit'-rai, scribe.
SHITTIM, shit'-tim, acacias.
SHIZA, shi'-za, beloved.
SHOAH, sho'-ah, opulent.
SHOBAB, sho'-bab, apostate.
SHOBACH, sho'-bak, pouring.
SHOBAI, sho'-bai, who leads many captive.
SHOHI, sho'-bi.

SHOBAL, sho'-bal, flowing, or a shoot.
SHOBEK, sho'-bek, forsaking.
SHOCHOH, sho'-ko, a hedge.
SHOHAM, sho'-ham, onyx, or sardonyx
SHOMER, sho'-mer, watchman.
SHOPHACH, sho'-fak, pouring.
SHOSHANNIM, shosh-an'-nim, lilies.
SHUA, shu'-ah, wealth.
SHUAH, shu'-ah, pit.
SHUAL, shu'-al.
SHUBAEL, shu'-ba-el.
SHUHAM, shu'-ham.
SHULAMITE, shu'-lam-ite.
SHUMATHITES, shu'-ma-thites, i.e., garlic.
SHUNEM, shu'-nem, two resting-places.
SHUNAMITE, shu'-na-mite.
SHUNI, shu'-ni, quiet.
SHUPHAM, shu'-pham, serpent.
SHUPPIM, shup'-pim, serpents.
SHUR, shur.
SHUSHAN, shu'-shan.
SHUTHELAH, shu-the'-lah, crashing or rending.
SIA, si'-a, council.
SIBBACHAI, sib'-ba-kai.
SIBBECAI, sib'-be-kai, } the wood
SIBBECHAI, sib'-be-kai, } of Jehovah, i.e., the crowd of the people of God.
SIBBOLETH, sib'-bo-leth (see SHIBBOLETH).
SIBMAH, sib'-mah, coolness, or sweet smell.
SIBRAIM, sib-ra'-im, twofold hope.
SICHEM, si'-kem.
SIDDIM, sid'-dim, valley of the plains.
SIDON, si'-don.
SIDONIANS, si-do'-ni-ans.
SIGIONETH, sig-yo'-neth.
SINHA, sin'-ha, council.
SIHON, si'-hon, sweeping away, i.e., a leader, carrying all before him.
SIHOR, si'-hor.
SILAS, si'-las, the third, considering.
SILLA, sil'-la, way, basket.
SILVANUS, sil-va'-nus, woody, or, of the forest.
SIMEON, sim'-e-on, hearing with acceptance.
SIMON, si'-mon.
SIMRI, sim'-ri, watchful.
SIN, sin, clay.
SINAI, si'-nai, the senna shrub.
SINA, si'-na.
SINITE, si'-nite.

SION, si'-on, lifted up.
SIPHMOTH, sif'-moth.
SIPPAI, sip'-pai.
SIRAH, si'-rah, withdrawing.
SIRION, si'-ri-on.
SISAMAI, sis-a-ma'-i.
SISERA, sis'-e-ra, a field of battle.
SITNAH, sit'-nah, contention.
SIVAN, si'-van.
SMYRNA, smir'-nah.
So, so (Hebrew form of Egyptian word Sevech).
SOCHO, so'-ko, ⎫
SOCHOH, so'-ko, ⎬ a hedge.
SOCOH, so'-ko, ⎭
SODI, so'-di, an acquaintance of God.
SODOM, sod'-om, burning, conflagration.
SOLOMON, sol'-o-mon, preamble.
SOPATER, so'-pa-ter, father saved.
SOPHERETH, so'-fe-reth, scribe.
SOREK, so'-rek, choice vine.
SOSIPATER, so-sip'-a-ter, saving the father.
SOSTHENES, sos'-then-eez, strong, saviour.
SOTAI, so'-tai, deviator.
STACHYS, stak'-kis, an ear of corn.
STEPHEN, ste'-ven, ⎫ a crown, or
STEPHANAS, stef'-a-nas, ⎬ crowns.
SUAH, su'-ah, sweepings.
SUCCOTH, suk'-koth, booths.
SUCCOTH-BENOTH, suk'-koth-ben'-oth, booths of daughters.
SUCHATHITES, suk'-a-thites (not known).
SUKKIIMS, suk'-ki-ims, dwellers in tents.
SUR, sur, removed.
SUSANCHITES, su-san'-kites, inhabitants of Susa or Shushan.
SUSANNAH, su-san'-nah, lily, rose, or joy.
SUSI, su'-si, horseman.
SYCHAR, si'-kar, drunken.
SYCHEM, si'-kem, Shechem.
SYENE, si-e'-ne, opening, key (i. e., of Egypt).
SYNTYCHE, sin'-ty-kee, affable.
SYRIA, sir'-i-a (not known).
SYRIAN, sir'-i-an, inhabitant of Syria.
SYRACUSE, si'-ra-kuse (not known).
SYROPHENICIAN, si'-ro-fee-nish-yan, Phenicians living in Syria.

TAANACH, ta'-a-nak, sandy soil, approach to Shiloh.

TAANATH-SHILOH, ta'-a-nath-shi'-lo.
TABBAOTH, tab'-ba-oth, rings.
TABBATH, tab'-bath, renowned.
TABEAL, tab'-e-al, ⎫ the goodness of
TABEEL, tab'-e-el, ⎬ God; or, God is good.
TABERAH, tab'-e-rah, burning.
TABITHA, tab'-i-thah, gazelle.
TABOR, ta'-bor, a lofty place, mound.
TABRIMON, tab'-ri-mon, who pleases Rimmon, for Rimmon is good.
TACHMONITE, tak'-mo-nite (see HACHMONITE.)
TADMOR, tad'-mor, city of palms.
TAHAN, ta'-han, a camp, a station.
TAHANITES, ta'-han-ites, descendants of T.
TAHAPANES, ta-hap'-pa-nes, ⎫ head
TAHPENES, tah'-pen-es, ⎬ of the age or world.
TAHATH, ta'-hath, station, place.
TAHREA, tah-re'-a, cunning.
TAHTIM-HODSHI, tah'-tim-hod'-shi, nether land newly inhabited.
TALMAI, tal'-mai, abounding in furrows.
TALMON, tal'-mon, oppressed.
TAMAH, ta'-mah, laughter.
TAMAR, ta'-mar, a palm tree.
TAMMUZ, tam'-muz, terror (?)
TANACH, ta'-nak, sandy soil.
TANHUMETH, tan-hu'-meth, consolation.
TAPHATH, ta'-fath, a drop.
TAPPUAH, tap'-pu-ah, a place fruitful in apples.
TARAH, ta'-rah, station.
TARALAH, tar'-a-lah, reeling.
TARHEA, ta-re'-a (see TAHREA.)
TARPELITES, tar'-pe-lites (unknown).
TARSHISH, tar'-shish, hard ground (?)
TARSUS, tar'-sus (probably same as TARSHISH).
TARTAK, tar'-tak, profound darkness, or hero of darkness.
TARTAN, tar'-tan, military chief.
TATNAI, tat'-nai, gift.
TEBAH, te'-bah, slaughter, executioner.
TEBALIAH, teb-a-li'-ah, one whom Jehovah has immersed (i. e., purified.)
TEBETH, te'-beth (unknown.)
TEHINNAH, te-hin'-nah, cry for mercy.
TEKEL, te'-kel, winged.
TEKOA, te-ko'-a, ⎫ pitching of
TEKOAH, te-ko'-ah, ⎬ tents.

TEKOITES, te-ko'-ites, inhabitants of T.

TEL-ABIB, tel-a'-bib, hill of ears of corn.

TELAH, te'-lah, fracture.

TELAIM, te-la'-im, young lambs.

TELASSAR, te-las'-sar, hill of Assar (?)

TELEM, te'-lem, oppression.

TEL-HARSA, tel-har-'sah,
TEL-HARESHA, tel-har'-e-sha, } hill of the wood.

TEL-MELAH, tel-me'-lah, hill of salt.

TEMA, te'-mah,
TEMAN, te'-man, } a desert, south.

TEMANI, te'-ma-ni,
TEMANITE, te'-ma-nite, } descendants of T.

TERAH, te'-rah, a station.

TERAPHIM, ter'-a-fim, prosperous life (?)

TERESH, te'-resh, severe, austere.

TERTIUS, ter'-shi-us, the third.

TERTULLUS, ter'-tul-lus, diminution of T.

THADDEUS, thad-de'-us, praising, confessing.

THAHASH, tha'-hash, badger or seal.

THAMAH, tha'-mah, laughter.

THARAH, tha'-rah (see TERAH.)

THEBEZ, the'-bez, brightness.

THELASAR, thel-as'-ar (see TELASSAR.

THEOPHILUS, the-off'-i-lus, lover of God.

THESSALONICA, thes-a-lo-ni'-ka.

THEUDAS, thew'-das, praise, confession.

THIMNATHAH, thim-na'-tha, portion assigned.

THOMAS, tom'-as, a twin, sound.

THUMMIM, thum'-mim, truth.

THYATIRA, thi-a-ti'-rah (unknown.)

TIBERIAS, ti-be'-ri-as (named after Tiberias).

TIBERIUS, ti-be'-ri-us, son of the river Tiber.

TIBHATH, tib'-hath, butchery.

TIBNI, tib'-ni, building of Jehovah.

TIDAL, ti'-dal, fear, reverence.

TIGLATH-PILESER, tig'-lath-pi-lo'-zer,
TIGLATH-PILNESER, tig'-lath-pil-ne'-zer, } lord of the Tigris.

TIKVAH, tik'-vah,
TIKVATH, tik-vath, } expectation.

TILON, ti'-lon, gift.

TIMEUS, ti-me'-us, polluted (?)

TIMNA, tim'-na,
TIMNAH, tim'-nah,
TIMNATH, tim'-nath, } restraint, restrained.

TIMNATH-HERES, tim'-nath-he'-res, portion of the sun.

TIMNATH-SERAH, tim'-nath-se'-rah, abundant portion.

TIMON, ti'-mon, burning.

TIMOTHEUS, ti-mo'-the-us,
TIMOTHY, tim'-o-thy, } honour of God.

TIPHSAH, tif'-sah, passage, ford.

TIRAS, ti'-ras, desire.

TIRATHITES, ti'-ra-thites (unknown).

TIRHAKAH, tir'-ha-kah, exalted.

TIRHANAH, tir'-ha-nah, scourge.

TIRIA, tir'-i-a, fear.

TIRZAH, tir'-zah, pleasantness.

TISHBITE, tish'-bite, inhabitant of Tishbe.

TISRI, or TIZRI, tiz'-ri, expiation (?) beginning (?)

TITUS, ti'-tus, honourable.

TOAH, to'-ah, inclined, lowly.

TOB, tob, good.

TOB-AD-ONIJAH, tob-ad-o-ni'-jah, good is my lord Jehovah.

TOBIAH, to-bi'-ah,
TOBIJAH, to-bi'-jah, } pleasing to J.

TOCHEN, to'-ken, a measure.

TOGARMAH, to-gar'-mah, breaking bones (?)

TOHU, to'-hu (same as TOAH).

TOI, to'-i,
TOU, to'-u, } error.

TOLA, to'-la, worm.

TOLAD, to'-lad, race, posterity, birth.

TOPHEL, to'-fel, lime, cement.

TOPHET, to'-fet, tabret-grove (?)

TRACHONITIS, trak-o-ni'-tis, stray.

TROAS, tro'-as (unknown).

TROGYLLIUM, tro-gil'-li-um.

TROPHIMUS, trof'-i-mus, nourished.

TRYPHENA, tri-fe'-nah, delicious.

TRYPHOSA, tri-fo'-sah, thrice shining, living delicately.

TUBAL, tu'-bal, flowing forth.

TUBALCAIN, tu'-bal-kane, worker in ore.

TYCHICUS, tik'-i-kus, fortunate.

TYRANNUS, ti-ran'-nus, reigning, prince.

TYRE, tire,
TYRUS, ti'-rus, } rock.

UCAL, u'-kal, I shall prevail.
UEL, u'-el, will of God.
ULAI, u-la'-i, strong water (?)
ULAM, u'-lam, infant.
ULLA, ul'-la, yoke.
UMMAH, um'-mah, community.
UNNI, un'-ni, depressed.
UPHAZ, u'-faz (perhaps OPHIR).
UPHARSIN, u-far'-sin.
UR, ur, light (?)
URBANE, ur'-ban, civil, courteous, gentle in speech.
URI, u'-ri, fiery.
URIAH, u-ri'-ah, } flame of Jeho-
URIJAH, u-ri'-jah, } vah.
URIEL, u'-ri-el, flame of God.
URIM, u'-rim, lights.
UTHAI, u'-thai, whom Jehovah succours.
UZ, uz, soft and sandy earth (?) fertile land (?)
UZAI, u'-zai, robust.
UZAL, u'-zal, wanderer.
UZZA, } uz'-zah, strength.
UZZAH, }
UZZEN-SHERAH, uz'-zen-she'-rah, ear (or rather corner) of Sherah.
UZZI, uz'-zi } might of Jeho-
UZZIAH, uz-zi'-ah, } vah.
UZZIEL, uz'-zi-el, power of God.
UZZIELITES, uz'-zi-el-ites, descendants of Uzziel.

VAJEZATHA, va-jez-a'-tha, white, pure.
VANIAH, va-ni'-ah, weak.
VASHNI, vash'-ni (uncertain; probably not a proper name).
VASHTI, vash'-ti, beautiful woman.
VOPHSI, vof'-si, my addition.

ZAANAN, za'-a-nan, place of flocks.
ZAANANIM, za-a-nan'-im, } remov-
ZAANAIM, za-a-na'-im, } ings.
ZAAVAN, za'-a-van, disturbed.
ZABAD, za'-bad, gift.
ZABBAI, zab-ba'-i, pure.
ZABBUD, zab'-bud, given, a gift bestowed (i. e., by God).
ZABDI, zab'-di, the gift of Jehovah.
ZABDIEL, zab'-di-el, the gift of God.
ZABULON (see ZEBULON).
ZABUD, za'-bud (same as ZABBUD).
ZACCAI, zak-ka'-i, } pure, inno-
ZACCHEUS, zak-ke'-us, } cent.
ZACCHUR, zak'-kur, mindful.

ZACHARIAH, zak-a-ri'-ah, } whom
ZACHARIAS, zak-a-ri'-as, } Jehovah remembers.
ZACHER, za'-ker, memorial, praise.
ZADOK, za'-dok, just.
ZAHAM, za'-ham, loathing.
ZAIR, za'-ir, small.
ZALAPH, za'-laf, fracture, wound.
ZALMON, zal'-mon, } shady.
ZALMONAH, zal-mo'-nah, }
ZALMUNNA, zal-mun'-nah, to whom shadow is denied.
ZAM-ZUMMIMS, zam-zum'-mims, tribes making a noise.
ZANOAH, zan-o'-ah, marsh, bog.
ZAPHNATH-PAANEAH, zaf'-nath-pa-a-ne'-ah, preserver of the age.
ZAPHON, za'-fon, north.
ZARAH, za'-rah, a rising (of light).
ZAREAH, za'-re-ah, hornet's tower.
ZAREATHITES, za'-re-a-thites, inhabitants of Zareah.
ZARED, za'-red, exuberant growth.
ZAREPHATH, zar'-e-fath, workshop for melting and refining metals.
ZARETAN, zar'-e-tan, } cooling.
ZARTANAH, zar'-ta-nah, }
ZARETH-SHAHAR, za'-reth-sha'-har, the splendour of the morning.
ZARHITES, zar'-hites, descendants of Zerah.
ZATTHU, zat'-thu, } a sprout.
ZATTU, zat'-tu, }
ZAZA, za'-za, plenty (?)
ZEBAH, ze'-bah, slaughtering, sacrifice.
ZEBADIAH, zeb-a-di'-ah, the gift of Jehovah.
ZEBEDEE, zeb'-e-dee, J. gave.
ZEBINA, ze'-bi-nah, bought.
ZEBOIM, ze-bo'-im, hyænas.
ZEBUDAH, ze-bu'-dah, given.
ZEBUL, ze'-bul, }
ZEBULON, zeb'-u-lon, } habitation.
ZEBULUN, zeb'-u-lun, }
ZECHARIAH, zek-a-ri'-ah, whom Jehovah remembers.
ZEDAD, ze'-dad, a mountain, the side of a mountain.
ZEDEKIAH, zed-e-ki'-ah, justice of Jehovah.
ZEEB, ze'-eb, wolf.
ZELAH, ze'-lah, a rib, the side.
ZELEK, ze'-lek, fissure.
ZELOPHEHAD, ze-lof'-e-had, fracture, a first rupture, perhaps firstborn.

ZELOTES, ze-lo'-teez, jealous, or zealous.

ZELZAH, zel'-zah, shade in the heat of the sun.

ZEMARAIM, zem-a-ra'-im, double bell (?)

ZEMARITES, zem'-a-rites (unknown).

ZEMIRA, ze-mi'-rah, song.

ZENAN, ze-na'n, place of flocks.

ZENAS, ze'-nas, contraction of Zenodorus.

ZEPHANIAH, zef-a-ni'-ah, whom Jehovah hid (i.e., defended).

ZEPHATH, ze'-fath, } watch-
ZEPHATHAH, ze-fa'-thah, } tower.
ZEPHO, ze-fo',

ZEPHON, ze-fo'ne, a looking out.

ZEPHONITES, ze-fo'-nites, descendants of Zephon.

ZER, zer, narrow, flint.

ZERAH, ze'-rah, a rising (of light).

ZERAHIAH, zer-a-hi'-ah, whom Jehovah caused to rise.

ZERED, ze'-red, exuberant growth.

ZEREDA, ze-re'-dah, } cool-
ZEREDATHAH, ze-re-da'-thah, } ing.

ZERESH, ze'-resh, gold.

ZERETH, ze'-reth, splendour.

ZEROR, ze'-ror, bundle or purse.

ZERUAH, ze-ru'-ah, leprous.

ZERUBBABEL, ze-rub'-ba-bel, scattered to Babylon, or, born at Babylon.

ZERUIAH, zer-ew'-yah, cleft.

ZETHAM, ze'-tham, } olive.
ZETHAN, ze'-than, }

ZETHAR, ze'-thar, star.

ZIA, zi'-ah, motion.

ZIBA, zi'-bah, a plant, statue.

ZIBEON, zib'-e-on, }
ZIBIA, zib'-i-a, } dyed, roe.
ZIBIAH, zib-i'-ah, }

ZICHRI, zik'-ri, celebrated, famous.

ZIDDIM, zid'-dim, sides.

ZIDKIJAH, zid-ki'-jah, justice of Jehovah.

ZIDON, zi'-don, fishing.

ZIDONIANS, zi-do'-ni-ans, inhabitants of Zidon.

ZIF, zif, splendour.

ZIHA, zi'-ha, drought.

ZIKLAG, zik'-lag, outpouring.

ZILLAH, zil'-lah, shadow.

ZILPAH, zil'-pah, a dropping.

ZILTHAI, zil'-thai, shadow (i. e., protection of Jehovah).

ZIMMAH, zim'-mah, mischief.

ZIMRAM, zim'-ram, } celebrated in
ZIMRI, zim'-ri, } song.

ZIN, zin, a low palm tree.

ZINA, zi'-na, ornament (?)

ZION, zi'-on, a sunny plain, a sunny mountain.

ZIOR, zi'-or, smallness.

ZIPH, zif, borrowed, flowing.

ZIPHION, zif'-yon, expectation, looking out.

ZIPHRON, zif'-ron, sweet smell.

ZIPPOR, zip'-por, little bird.

ZIPPORAH, zip'-po-rah, fem. of Zippor.

ZITHRI, zith'-ri, protection of J.

ZIZ, ziz, a flower.

ZIZA, zi'-zah, } abundance.
ZIZAH, zi'-zah, }

ZOAN, zo'-an, low region.

ZOAR, zo'-ar, smallness.

ZOBA, zo'-bah, } a station.
ZOBAH, zo'-bah, }

ZOBEBAH, zo'-be-bah, walking slowly

ZOHAR, zo'-har, whiteness.

ZOHELETH, zo'-he-leth, serpent, stone of the serpent.

ZOHETH, zo'-heth (uncertain).

ZOPHAH, zo'-phah, cruse.

ZOPHAI, zo'-fai, honeycomb.

ZOPHAR, zo'-phar, sparrow.

ZOPHIM, zo'-fim, watchers.

ZORAH, zo'-rah, a place of hornets.

ZORATHITES, zo'-ra-thites, people of Zorah.

ZORITES, zo'-rites (same as ZORATHITES).

ZOROBABEL, zo-rob'-a-bel (see ZERUBBABEL).

ZUAR, zu'-ar, smallness.

ZUPH, zuf, flag, sedge.

ZUR, zur, rock, shape, form.

ZURIEL, zu'-ri-el, whose rock is God.

ZURISHADDAI, zu'-ri-shad'-dai, whose rock is the Almighty.

ZUZIMS, zu'-zims, sprouting, or restless.

TABLES OF TIME, MEASURES, WEIGHTS, &c.

SACRED YEAR.		CIVIL YEAR.	
Names and Order of the Hebrew Months.		*Names and Order of the Hebrew Months.*	
1. Nisan, answering to part of......	March. April.	7.—1. Tizri, answering to part of	September. October.
2. Zif or Jiar	April. May.	8.—2. Marchesvan.	October. November.
3. Sivan	May. June.	9.—3. Chisleu	November. December.
4. Thamuz	June. July.	10.—4. Tebeth	December. January.
5. Ab	July. August.	11.—5. Shebat	January. February.
6. Elul	August. September.	12.—6. Adar	February. March.
7. Ethanim or Tizri	September. October.	1.—7. Nisan	March. April.
8. Marchesvan or Bul	October. November.	2.—8. Zif or Jiar .	April. May.
9. Chisleu............	November. December.	3.—9. Sivan	May. June.
10. Tebeth	December. January.	4.—10. Thamuz ..	June. July.
11. Shebat	January. February.	5.—11. Ab	July. August.
12. Adar...............	February. March.	6.—12. Elul.........	August. September.
13. Ve-Adar or Second Adar.			

The Jews reckoned their months according to the moon: and every third year they added a month, which they called Ve-Adar, in the same way as we add a day in every fourth or leap year.

They began their civil year in the month Tizri, or September, according to which they computed and settled all temporal affairs. But after coming out of Egypt they began their ecclesiastical year in the month of Nisan, or March, from which they computed all their great festivals.

Their day was twofold: the *natural*, consisting of twenty-four hours, which commenced at sunset; and the *artificial*, beginning at sunrising and ending at sunset, which was divided into twelve equal parts or hours. See John xi. 9.

Their night was divided into four parts or watches, each consisting of three hours. The first began at sunset; the second at nine o'clock; the third at midnight; the fourth at three in the morning, and continued until sunrise. These were sometimes otherwise expressed; viz., *even*, *midnight, cock-crowing*, and the *dawn*. See Mark xiii. 35.

Their artificial day was divided into four equal parts. The first began at sunrise, and continued until nine o'clock; the second began at nine, and continued till noon; the third began at noon, and ended at three in the afternoon (which is sometimes termed the ninth hour); the fourth began at three, and continued till sunset.

Our Saviour was seized in the garden some, time after midnight, or during the third watch. Then He was hurried first to the palace of Caiaphas, where Peter denied Him. Afterwards the rest of the priests, scribes, and the whole council began to assemble in the dawn, or before sunrising. Their examination of Him, and bringing Him before Pilate, lasted till nine o'clock. From thence to noon they were employed in preparing for His execution, and conducting Him to Calvary. He was affixed on the cross at noon, which is sometimes termed the sixth hour. He continued on it in agony until three in the afternoon, at which time precisely He expired. This was the hour when the paschal lamb which typified Him used to be slain.

A TABLE OF MEASURES.

A Cubit, somewhat more than one foot nine inches English.
A Span, half a cubit, or nearly eleven inches.
A Hand-breadth, sixth part of a cubit, or a little more than three inches and a half.
A Fathom, four cubits, about seven feet three inches and a half.
A Measuring Reed, six cubits and a hand-breadth, or nearly eleven feet. This was used in measuring buildings.
A Measuring Line, fourscore cubits, about one hundred and forty-five feet eleven inches. This was used to measure grounds; hence *the lines* (Psa. xvi. 6) are taken figuratively for the inheritance itself.
A Stadium or Furlong, nearly 146 paces.
A Sabbath day's Journey, about 729 paces.
An Eastern Mile, one mile and 403 paces, English measure.
A Day's Journey, upwards of thirty-three miles and a half.
Note.—A pace is equal to five feet.
There were different kinds of cubits. The common cubit, called the cubit of a man (Deut. iii. 11), was about eighteen inches. The king's cubit was three inches longer than the common one. The holy cubit was a yard, or two common ones.

A TABLE OF WEIGHTS.

A Shekel, near half an ounce, Troy weight.
A Maneh, was sixty shekels, about two pounds and a quarter.
A Talent, three thousand shekels, or 113 pounds, and upwards, of ten ounces.

A TABLE OF MONEY.

	£	s.	d.
A Shekel of Gold, worth about	1	16	5¼
A Golden Daric, about	1	1	10
A Talent of Gold, about	5,464	5	8
A Shekel of Silver, about	0	2	3¼
A Bekah, half a shekel, about	0	1	2
A Gerah, twentieth part of a shekel, about . . .	0	0	1¼
A Maneh or Mina, fifty shekels	5	13	10
A Talent of Silver, 3,000 shekels, about . . .	341	10	5
A Silver Drachma, about	0	0	7¾
Tribute Money, two drachms	0	1	3¼
A Piece of Silver (*Stater*)	0	2	7
A Pound (*Mornai*), 100 drachms	3	4	7
A Roman Penny (*Denarius*)	0	0	7¾
A Farthing (*Assarium*), about	0	0	1¼

Another Farthing (*Quadrans*), half the former.

A Mite, the half of this latter.

Note.—Silver is here reckoned at five shillings per ounce, and gold at four pounds per ounce.

MEASURES OF LIQUIDS.

The Cor, or Chomer, seventy-five gallons and somewhat above five pints.

The Bath, the tenth of the chomer, or seven gallons four pints and a half.

The Hin, sixtieth of a chomer, about a gallon and a quart.

The Log, about three-fourths of a pint.

The Firkin (*Metretes*), somewhat more than seven pints.

MEASURES OF DRY THINGS.

The Cab, somewhat above two pints.

The Omer, above five pints.

The Seah, one peck and about half a pint.

The Ephah, three pecks and about three pints.

The Letech, about four bushels.

The Homer, about eight bushels.

The Chœnix (mentioned Rev. vi. 6) was the daily allowance to maintain a slave. It contained about a quart, some say only a pint and a half. When this measure was sold for a denarius, or Roman penny, corn must have been above twenty shillings an English bushel, which indicates a scarcity next to a famine.

N.B.—In the above tables of coins and measures the fractional parts are omitted, as exactness in this point would be of little use to the common English reader

Sunday School Union.

——⟶∘⟵——

EDUCATIONAL WORKS

FOR

TEACHERS AND BIBLE STUDENTS.

——⟶∘⟵——

Joshua and His Successors: An Introduction to the Books of Joshua, Judges, Ruth, and Samuel. With Notes, Critical and Illustrative, and Maps. By W. H. GROSER, B.Sc. (Lond.), Examiner in the Principles and Art of Teaching to the London Sunday School Union. Crown 8vo., cloth boards, marble edges, price 4s.; or in two parts, limp cloth, price 2s. each.

The Art of Teaching in a Sunday School. By J. G. FITCH, M.A., one of Her Majesty's Inspectors of Schools. Royal 18mo., cloth boards, 1s. Containing Three Lectures, respectively on Questioning, Attention, and Memory.

The Apostle Peter: His Life and Letters. By Rev. S. G. GREEN, D.D. Crown 8vo., cloth boards, red edges, price 3s.

The Geography of Palestine. By J. A. MEEN. An Historical and Descriptive Account of the Holy Land. Carefully compiled, revised, and adapted to recent Researches. Second Edition, price 2s. cloth; 2s. 6d. gilt edges.

An Introduction to the Knowledge of Holy Scripture. By Rev. SAMUEL GREEN. Fcap. 8vo., cloth boards, price 2s.

The Four Gospels and the One Christ. A Study and a Guide. By Rev. G. B. JOHNSON, of Edgbaston. Crown 8vo., cloth limp, price 1s. 6d.

SUNDAY SCHOOL UNION, 56, OLD BAILEY.

The Written Word; or, The Contents and Interpretation of Holy Scripture briefly considered. By Rev. SAMUEL G. GREEN, D.D. President of Rawdon College, Yorkshire. Fcap. 8vo., 1s. 6d. cloth boards.

Ready for Work; or, Hints on the Preparation of Bible Lessons. By W. H. GROSER, B.Sc., Author of "Bible Months," "Our Work," &c. &c. With Examples of Outline Lessons for all Grades of a Sunday School. Second Edition. Price 1s.

Review Exercises in the Sunday School. By Rev. H. C. TRUMBULL, Secretary of the American Sunday School Union. Royal 18mo., cloth boards, price 1s.

The Art of Picturing. By W. H. GROSER, B.Sc. (Lond.) Fcap. 8vo., paper covers, price 3d.

The Principles and Art of Teaching. A Lecture. By J. A. COOPER, Author of "Counsels to Sunday School Teachers." Paper covers, 3d.

Wagons for Eye-gate; or, Illustrative Teaching. By W. F. CRAFTS, of America. Price 3d.

Outlines of Scripture Geography. By Professor E. H. PALMER, M.A. Cloth, red edges, with Maps, price 8d.

The Biblical Treasury. Devoted exclusively to Biblical Illustration and Criticism, gathered from Oriental Customs, Natural History and Philosophy, Topography, Historic Events, Missionary Incidents, Idolatrous Usages, and the Facts of Every-day Life. 15 vols., price 1s. 8d. each; or in 7 double vols., price 3s. each; extra bound for Presentation and other purposes, in half-calf, 6s. per double vol.; half-morocco, 6s. 6d. Classified Index to the first 6 vols., price 8d.

SUNDAY SCHOOL UNION, 56, OLD BAILEY.

The Teacher's Companion. Designed to exhibit the Principles of Sunday School Instruction and Discipline. By R. N. COLLINS. With an Introductory Essay by Rev. DANIEL MOOR, M.A. Fcap. 8vo., cloth boards. New Edition. Price 4s.

Our Work. By W. H. GROSER, B.Sc. (Lond.). Fourth Edition. Cloth, 1s. 6d.; gilt edges, 2s. Originally delivered as Lectures, containing : 1. Our Material; or, What is a Child? 2. The Instruments; or, What to Teach. 3. How to Teach: or, the Right Use of the Instruments. 4. At Work : The Teacher Teaching.

The Sunday School. By Mrs. DAVIDS. 12mo., cloth, price 3s. A Prize Essay, giving a general view of Sunday Schools as an agency of the Church, adapted for the improvement of the young; on the formation and management of Sunday Schools; the conduct of classes; and directions to junior teachers.

Todd's Sunday School Teacher. A Manual for Sunday School Teachers. By Rev. JOHN TODD. Cloth boards, 2s.; gilt edges, 2s. 6d. Designed to aid in elevating and perfecting the Sunday School System.

The Infant Class in the Sunday School. By SIR CHARLES REED, F.S.A. Cloth boards, 1s. 6d.

The Young Men's Class. By W. S. BLACKET. New Edition. Fcap. 8vo., cloth boards, 1s. 6d. ; gilt, 2s.

Papers for Teachers on the various Departments of Sunday Schools and Sunday School Work. Cloth boards, 1s. 6d.

Senior Classes in Sunday Schools. By W. H. WATSON. Limp cloth, price 6d.

The Sunday School Hand-Book. Limp cloth, price 8d. Containing directions for the establishment and management of Sunday Schools, with ground plans and explanatory tables.

Teacher-Training : Suggestions on the Formation and Conduct of Training and Normal Classes in Sunday Schools. By W. H. GROSER, B.Sc. (Lond.). Price 3d.

SUNDAY SCHOOL UNION, 56, OLD BAILEY.

Bible Months; or, The Seasons in Palestine, as illustrative of Scripture. By W. H. GROSER, B.Sc. 2nd Edition, price 1s. 6d. cloth; gilt edges. An attempt to exhibit, in the form of a Monthly Calendar, the aspect of the country, and the occupations of its inhabitants different seasons of the year. With a Map and many Illustrations.

The Introductory Class Book. By B. P. Pask. Cloth, edges, price 3s. 6d. A Course of Study for intending Sunday School Teachers.

The Good Steward. By THULIA S. HENDERSON (Mrs. ENGALL). A Manual for Teachers (Prize Essay). Fcap. 8vo., cloth 1s. 6d.; gilt edges. Part 1. The Teacher's Personal Characteristics.—Part The Teacher's Official Qualifications.—Part 3. The Teacher's Actual Labours.—Part 4. The Teacher's Relative Duties.

Paul the Apostle. Fcap. 8vo., cloth, 1s. Containing Scenes from his Life, Labours, and Travels, and Maps.

Pictorial Description of the Tabernacle. Crown 8vo., price 2d. This valuable little work was prepared by the late DILWORTH, Esq., and describes the Rites and Ceremonies connected with the Tabernacle Service.

Counsels to Sunday School Teachers on Personal Improvement and Practical Efficiency. By J. A. COOPER, of Birmingham. Cl., 2

Hours with My Class. By the late W. GOVER. A Series of Specimen Lessons. 18mo., cloth boards, 1s.

Addresses to Children. By the Rev. S. G. GREEN, D.D. Cloth boards, 1s. each.

Addresses to Children, with Introductory Observations to Ministers and Teachers.

Twelve Lectures to Children on the Bible.
Twelve Lectures to Children on Bible Doctrines.

Printed in the USA
CPSIA information can be obtained
at www.ICGtesting.com
LVHW011505061023
760360LV00003B/10